WHAT EVERY MAN WANTS

THE ULTIMATE TROPHY BOOK

ANDREW MANN

INTRODUCED BY

FRANKIE DETTORI MBE

ICON BOOKS

Published in the UK in 2006
by Icon Books Ltd, The Old Dairy,
Brook Road, Thriplow,
Cambridge SG8 7RG
email: info@iconbooks.co.uk
www.iconbooks.co.uk

Sold in the UK, Europe, South Africa and Asia
by Faber & Faber Ltd, 3 Queen Square,
London WC1N 3AU
~ or their agents

Distributed in the UK, Europe, South Africa and Asia
by TBS Ltd, TBS Distribution Centre, Colchester Road
Frating Green, Colchester CO7 7DW

Published in Australia in 2006
by Allen & Unwin Pty Ltd,
PO Box 8500, 83 Alexander Street,
Crows Nest, NSW 2065

Distributed in Canada by
Penguin Books Canada,
90 Eglinton Avenue East, Suite 700,
Toronto, Ontario M4P 2YE

ISBN-10: 1-84046-775-4
ISBN-13: 978-1840467-75-8

Typesetting and design by Andrew Mann

Printed and bound in the UK by Mackays of Chatham

CONTENTS

INTRODUCTION

I know what *I* want. I want to win, be the best at what I do, and then get my hands on a trophy or two for doing it. Trophies are great. They are essential to the whole magic of sport and of winning; they first underline your victory, and then serve as a constant reminder of how hard you worked and what you achieved. And what better way to remember than by looking at a beautifully crafted and glistening bit of silver or gold!

Although I've won a lot in horse racing, I've always wondered what it would be like to be at the top of other sports and get my hands on their most hallowed trophies as well. I'd be lying if I said I hadn't dreamt of leading my beloved Arsenal to victory in the FA Cup. Thierry and I would make a mean partnership up front, I know it!

Maybe one day I'll get to kiss that Claret Jug, having just got the better of Tiger in a play-off in the Open Championship. Actually, it wouldn't go to a play-off, I'm sure I'd have it all wrapped up way before then!

I also suspect I'd look rather dapper in the Tour de France's Yellow Jersey, as long as they had it in my size of course! Having said that, I think I'll stick to riding horses for the time being – riding a bike for more than 2,000 miles over three weeks strikes me as a little too much hard work for my liking.

What Every Man Wants is the ultimate guide to the world's most sought-after sporting prizes. For each trophy, it gives you the essential facts, histories, memorable moments and more. This book is for all men who love a bit of sport, including myself, who have dreamed about winning their favourite competitions. We're all the same. We grew up watching our sporting heroes celebrating with the famous cups and prizes that at some point we've also imagined as our own. On some occasions, it still gets a little too much for me, though. In the lead-up to the World Cup final earlier in the summer, I could barely sleep. But once Italy won ... I slept like a baby for weeks, imagining myself at Rome's Circus Maximus cheekily grabbing that wonderful gold trophy from my Italian team-mates and raising it aloft in front of the million fans who had come to help us celebrate winning football's holy grail. It'll never change – I'll always think like that, and I'll always love trophies.

And so, believing trophies to be as important as I do, I've had a very sad time recently trying to come to terms with a great loss in my life. As you might have read or heard in the news, I've had a number of my most prized racing trophies stolen. As if that wasn't bad enough, the thief also made off with my MBE medal, which I proudly received from the Queen in 2000. If I didn't know how much they meant to me before, I certainly do now. Losing these magical items has left me feeling utterly deflated – they represented the triumphs of my career and constantly reminded me of those. Of course, the memories of crossing the line first in those races can never really be taken away from me, but I'm pretty sure my trophies are far more significant to me than to whoever has them now.

I can only hope that by the time this goes to print, my trophies and MBE will have been returned, but I'm not holding my breath. If there is one upside to this horrible incident, it's that I'm now more determined than ever to win more trophies to take their place. And you never know, I just might set my sights on the FA Cup! The only problem is trying to get Arsène to pick me …

Frankie Dettori MBE
September 2006

THE ASHES

THE ASHES

AWARDED FOR WINNING:

The world's greatest and most historical biennial Test cricketing clash. Otherwise known as The Ashes.

CONTESTED BY:

Australia and England.

A BRIEF HISTORY:

'In affectionate remembrance of English cricket, which died at The Oval, 29 August 1882. Deeply lamented by a large circle of sorrowing friends and acquaintances, RIP. N.B. The body will be cremated and the Ashes taken to Australia.'

The first Test match between the two countries had been played in 1877, but it was their ninth Test, and Australia's first and unexpected victory on English soil over a full-strength English side in 1882, that inspired a young British journalist, Reginald Shirley Brooks, to write this obituary in the *Sporting Times*.

A subsequent trip to Australia had already been organised prior to England's seven-run defeat, so three weeks later a team led by the Honourable Ivo Bligh set sail. Their objective was, as the English media put it, 'recovering the Ashes'. Although Australia hammered England in the first Test by nine wickets, England won the following two and so achieved their goal. This prompted a group of ladies from Melbourne to put some ashes in a small brown urn and present them to Bligh, saying: 'What better way than to actually present the English captain with the very object, albeit mythical, he had come to Australia to retrieve?'

For over a hundred years it was believed that the urn contained the ashes of a bail used in the third match, but in 1998 Bligh's 82-year-old daughter-in-law created considerable debate with the claim that they were the remains of her mother-in-law's veil instead. If that daughter-in-law and mother-in-law bit sounds confusing, it's because Bligh had gone on to marry one of the Melbourne women. In any case, other evidence also surfaced suggesting that it was the ashes of a ball. So, although the origin of the actual Ashes is the subject of some dispute, the passion with which they are contested has never been in question.

MOST MEMORABLE MOMENTS:

■ In 1930 Australia toured England and won the Ashes with the brilliant Don Bradman scoring a ridiculous 974 runs across the series, a record that still remains today. Subsequently in 1932, England captain Douglas Jardine devised a tactic that came to be known as 'Bodyline'. His fast bowlers would aim at the bodies of Australian batsmen in the hope that, while trying to defend themselves, they would provide relatively simple catches to the large number of fielders he had placed close in on the leg side. Successful as it was in that it halved Bradman's batting average and ensured that England won the Ashes, it also badly injured a number of other Australian batsmen and ultimately caused a full-on diplomatic crisis.

While Bradman did his best to counter Bodyline by stepping to the leg side and cutting the ball to the vacant off-side field (and was hit above the waist only once throughout the series), some of his team-mates fared rather worse. Things came to a head in Adelaide in the third Test, when English fast bowler Harold Larwood fractured Bert Oldfield's skull and hit Australian captain Bill Woodfull in the chest, just above the heart. When Jardine placed his fielders in Bodyline positions after Woodfull's injury there was almost a riot in the ground, with police having to protect the English players from the enraged spectators. 'I've not travelled 6,000 miles to make friends. I'm here to win the Ashes', was Jardine's later response.

In 2004, in a poll of cricket journalists, commentators and players, the Bodyline Series was ranked the most important event in cricket history.

■ The 1936–7 series in Australia saw Bradman captain the Australian side for the first time. People began to seriously question his appointment after England went 2-0 up in the series. Then Bradman chose to silence his critics. He scored 270, 212 and 169 in the next three Tests, with Australia winning all three.

It remains the only time in Ashes history that a team has won a five-match series having been two down.

■ In 1948, a 39-year-old Don Bradman led the Australian team on their first tour of England after the Second World War. His team became part of cricketing legend as 'The Invincibles', playing 36 matches including five Tests but remaining unbeaten on the tour. They won 27 matches, drawing only nine, including the 4-0 Ashes series victory.

At that time, no team had ever made more than 400 runs in the fourth innings of a Test match to win. At Headingley, The Invincibles did just that.

The final day of the Test started with England on 362 for 8. England captain Norman Yardley decided that his side should bat for ten minutes before declaring to add a few more runs and also give himself the choice of roller between innings. He chose the heavy roller so as to break up the pitch and help his brilliant off-spinner Jim Laker. And so the scene was set; Australia required 404 runs to win in just 344 minutes.

Initially they fell behind, scoring just 32 in 45 minutes, before Lindsay Hassett was caught and bowled by Denis Compton, bringing Bradman to the crease. At lunch Australia were 121 for 1. Then came the onslaught. Arthur Morris and Bradman set about the English bowlers, hammering 301 runs in 217 minutes for the second wicket. Morris lost his wicket for 182 but Bradman, unbeaten on 173, guided them to their world-record target with ten minutes to spare. It was perhaps the most awesome display of batting Leeds will ever see.

■ The 1948 series is also known for one of the most poignant moments in Ashes history – in the fifth and final Test at The Oval, Bradman came to the crease for his last-ever Test innings, needing only four runs to retire with a career batting average of over 100. The English captain Norman Yardley called for three cheers for Bradman, and then shook him by the hand. Noticeably moved by the reception, Bradman took some time to compose himself before settling over his bat to face leg-spinner Eric Hollies.

Bradman played the first ball defensively, later saying that he hardly saw it, so stirred were his emotions. Hollies then bowled a googly at Bradman on a perfect length. Bradman went forward and got an inside edge on to his stumps. Unthinkably, Bradman was out, and his duck left him with a career average of 99.94.

It is, however, probably the only duck in cricketing history upon which the batsman has received a standing ovation from the entire ground on his return to the pavilion. They said goodbye to the greatest batsman that has ever lived.

■ In the Old Trafford Test in 1956, Jim Laker bowled 68 of England's 191 overs in the match. With it, he took nineteen of the twenty possible Australian wickets – a record that probably will never be surpassed.

Driving himself back to Surrey after the game, he stopped to refresh himself in a pub on the way. Customers were watching repeats of his performance on a TV, so he joined them to watch but went unrecognised. Once he was done, he quietly left, no one realising whose company they had just been in.

■ On 31 July 1975, a relatively unknown, bespectacled and grey-haired man in a jockey-peaked cap walked out to bat for England at Lord's for the very first time. (He had kept them waiting, however, as such was the occasion that David Steele had descended too many flights of stairs when leaving the pavilion and found himself in the basement toilets.) Without the protective gear available to players today, and with just a dressing room towel stuffed down his trousers as a thigh pad, the Englishman's first experience of Test cricket was to be the pace onslaught of Australian legends Dennis Lillee and Jeff Thomson. They had just ripped through the England batting line-up at Edgbaston and so far hadn't shown much evidence of relinquishing their grip here.

'Who the hell is this? Groucho Marx?', one of the

short-leg fielders asked as Steele arrived at the crease. 'Mornin'', offered the Englishman in response, before going on to make 50 in the first innings and 45 in the second.

■ The 1981 series, or 'Botham's Ashes' as it came to be known, saw probably the greatest comeback in Test history. At Headingley, in the third Test, England were made to follow on, being 227 runs behind. Famously, an English bookmaker offered odds of 500-1 for an English victory, upon which Australian players Dennis Lillee and Rod Marsh peculiarly laid a small bet. England, reduced to 135 for 7 in their second innings, looked like they were heading for a crushing defeat. Instead, they put on 221 for the last three wickets, Botham finishing on an unbeaten 149 and leaving Australia 130 to chase. A piece of cake for a team who were already leading the series 1-0, most would have thought. The Australians weren't counting on Willis taking 8 for 43, however, and they were dismissed for 111, giving England a miraculous victory by eighteen runs. Lillee and Marsh might have won some money, but that was scant consolation for the pain inflicted by such a defeat.

■ In 1985, when the two sides met at Edgbaston in the fifth Test, the series still hung in the balance at 1-1. Ian Botham scored only eighteen runs in the match, but they were rather special. When he arrived at the crease he immediately had to face the hostile pace bowling of a young and fired-up Craig McDermott. The first delivery was fast, straight and on a good length, and was despatched back over McDermott's head high up into the stand. The second was another boundary, this time for four, and the fourth despatched into the crowd, very much like the first.

■ You might think it somewhat difficult to pick out the single best delivery in a hundred years of cricket. Nevertheless, it's almost unanimously agreed that the 'Ball of the Century' came at Old Trafford in the first Ashes Test of 1993 – and more importantly, came from a hand delivering its first-ever ball in Ashes cricket.

After a slow and short run-up, a young and unknown Australian leg-spinner named Shane Warne arrived at the crease to deliver what appeared to be a normal leg-break to the facing right-handed Mike Gatting. It turned out to be anything but.

At first, it flew straight, but about halfway down the pitch the inordinate spin on the ball caused it to drift to the right. As the ball arrived at Gatting, it dipped suddenly before pitching well outside his leg stump. Having successfully followed the ball's deviation down the leg side, Gatting knew he couldn't be out lbw, and so pushed his bat and pad forward into a conventional position to defend a leg-break of this kind. If it didn't hit his pad, then his straight bat would be in place to act as a second line of defence. Instead, the ball bit on the turf and spun back so much that it missed absolutely everything except Gatting's off-stump.

No one could quite believe what they had just seen, least of all Gatting who – according to his captain Graham Gooch who was batting at the other end – 'looked as though someone had just nicked his lunch'. As the Aussies celebrated around him, Gatting just stood there before finally setting off on his long walk back to the pavilion, most of which he spent shaking his head in sheer disbelief at it all. You can hardly blame him though: he'd just faced the best delivery in 93 years.

■ The summer of 2005 in England saw what is widely regarded as the greatest Ashes series ever. With the destination of the little urn still undecided on the last day of the fifth and final Test, the outcome seemed to swing very much Australia's way as Kevin Pietersen (England's No. 5) came to the crease with Glenn McGrath on a hat-trick. Narrowly surviving an appeal for caught behind from his first ball, and despite it being his debut Test series, he launched one of the fiercest counter-attacks the Ashes had ever seen, leathering 158 including seven sixes (an Ashes record in an innings), to save the match and win back the Ashes for England. A hero, albeit with a stupid hairdo, was born.

IT'S BEEN WON THE MOST TIMES BY:

Australia with 30 series victories versus England's 28. Five of the 63 rubbers have been drawn, which resulted in Australia, as the current holders of the time, retaining the Ashes four times versus England's one.

IT'S MADE OF:

Terracotta, wood, paper and ash.

HEIGHT:

10 cm.

MANTELPIECE KUDOS:

Amazing in a fairly understated four-inch-tall-urn-type-way, although it probably means you've nicked it, as it's not meant to leave the MCC Museum at Lord's. Having said that, the Queen took it with her when she visited Australia for the country's bicentennial in 1988. As England had just won the Ashes in the previous year, that could only be described as her showing off a bit.

INSURANCE VALUE:

£1 million.

CLEANING/MAINTENANCE REQUIRED:

Some light dusting with Merv Hughes's moustache would be good. Some gentle buffing with W.G. Grace's beard would be perfect.

ESSENTIAL FACTS:

■ In 1877, Australia played England at Melbourne Cricket Ground and won by 45 runs. Exactly 100 years later they played a celebratory Centenary Test at the same ground and Australia won again by the same margin of 45 runs. Weird.

■ Don Bradman honed his skills as a child by hitting a golf ball against a brick wall in his backyard for hours on end with a cricket stump. Sounds easy, doesn't it? It's not.

■ Different players handle themselves while out in the middle in different ways. Former England captain Michael Atherton wrote in his autobiography of fellow former captain, Australian Steve Waugh: 'We decided at Old Trafford [during the 1997 Ashes series] not to sledge Waugh or engage him in any way. We felt he revelled in a hostile atmosphere and sledging merely fuelled his adrenalin. He arrived at the crease and soon realised this: "OK, you're not talking to me are you? Well, I'll talk to myself then." And he did, for 240 minutes in the first innings, and 382 minutes in the second.'

■ In 1989, Australian batsman David Boon reputedly drank 52 cans of beer on the flight to England for the Ashes tour. Apparently he was afraid of flying. Anyway, it didn't seem to cause any lasting damage, as he averaged 55 with the bat on the tour and helped his side win back the Ashes for the first time in five years.

The story goes that after landing, the Australian coach Bob Simpson called a team meeting: 'Righto, a couple of things: David, I'm very disappointed with you and you're on probation, but I also don't want this to leave the room. It's not to leave the Australian cricket team.' At which point Merv Hughes at the back put up his hand and said: 'Oh, Bob, I'm sorry mate, I've done radio interviews with ...' and rattled off four or five stations he'd already told. As everyone started to laugh, Hughes found himself on probation as well.

■ In 1990, England went to Australia for the Ashes. Although two down after three Tests,

David Gower was in great form, scoring centuries in both the second and third Tests. Before the fourth Test, England headed to the Carrara Oval for a match against Queensland. It turned out to be their only first-class win of the tour, and on the third day, English batsman John Morris completed a century before losing his wicket within minutes of Gower shortly before lunch.

Everyone had got used to the biplanes flying high above the ground throughout the match, and were aware of the airfield nearby. With the England side four wickets down at the time, Gower and Morris decided during lunch that it was safe to slip out of the ground and pay the airfield a visit. After checking on the radio that no more wickets had fallen, they both climbed into pre-war Tiger Moth biplanes and took off.

Once properly airborne, the planes were meant to stay over 2,000 feet, but Gower and Morris somehow persuaded their pilots to buzz the Oval at nearer 200. Allan Lamb, to whom Gower had quietly mentioned their intentions before leaving the ground, was out in the middle and playfully pretended to shoot them down with his bat. No one else had any idea.

■ From 1989 to the start of the series in 2005, 43 Ashes Tests were contested. Australia won 28 of them, England seven, and there were eight draws. More importantly, however, only one of England's seven victories (the first Test in 1997) was achieved when the Ashes was still at stake.

■ Australian Captain Allan Border's way of ingratiating himself to journalists during a press conference while on Tour in 1993: 'I am not talking to anyone in the British media ... they are all pricks.'

■ In 2001, Englishman Karl Power became famous overnight when, wearing the correct strip, he walked out onto the Olympic Stadium pitch in Munich with his Manchester United 'team-mates' and lined up next to Andy Cole for the pre-match team photograph before their Champions League quarter-final.

Later that year on the Friday of the Headingley Test, he was at it again. 'I'd hid in the toilets for two hours and the plan was to go out at the fall of a wicket before the incoming batsman', Power said. 'But my mobile rang at the wrong time and when I'd finished talking, Hussain was already out there.' It still seemed to work, though, as Power was again clad in all the correct kit including a helmet, and people thought Hussain must have been injured and come out with a runner.

When he removed his helmet it became apparent that he was an impostor, prompting one of the BBC Test Match Special commentary team to suggest: 'He is not the only one to masquerade as an England batsman.'

■ The quickest Ashes century was hit by Englishman Gilbert Jessop at The Oval in 1902. It took him just 75 minutes. As somewhat of a contrast, his later compatriot Geoff Miller took over two hours to make 7 on the 1978–9 trip to Australia.

■ The highest Ashes innings total is England's 903 for 7 declared at The Oval in 1938.

■ The lowest Ashes innings total is Australia's 36 all out at Edgbaston in 1902.

■ When England made Australia follow on at Trent Bridge in 2005, it was the first time they had suffered such ignominy in 191 Tests!

■ Australians have scored 264 centuries in Ashes Tests, 23 of them double centuries, while Englishmen have managed just 212 centuries, with only ten of them being converted into double centuries.

■ Australian bowlers have taken ten wickets in a match 41 times, while English bowlers are just behind, having achieved the feat on 38 different occasions.

■ During the Lord's Test in 1953, Len Hutton and Denis Compton were on the receiving end of some pretty torrid bowling from Australian pacemen Ray Lindwall and Keith Miller. Several blows to the body later, Hutton decided to summon Compton down the pitch. Compton enthusiastically advanced towards Hutton, eager to hear his useful tactical advice. 'Must be a better way of earning a living than this', suggested Hutton, and walked back to face the next ball.

■ The following poem is on the side of the Ashes urn:

When Ivo goes back with the urn, the urn;
Studds, Steel, Read and Tylecote return, return;
The welkin will ring loud,
The great crowd will feel proud,
Seeing Barlow and Bates with the urn, the urn;
And the rest coming home with the urn.

BEST KEPT:

Beside the urn containing your grandfather.

THE FA CUP

THE FA CUP

The oldest, most prestigious and most widely-viewed domestic football competition in the world.

CONTESTED BY:

674 teams across England and Wales (although Cardiff City is the only non-English side to win it, way back in 1927).

A BRIEF HISTORY:

Having played in an inter-house knockout tournament as a boy at Harrow School, FA Honorary Secretary Charles Alcock maintained that the formula could work on a bigger scale, and so at a meeting on 20 July 1871 he proposed 'that a Challenge Cup should be established in connection with the Association, for which all clubs belonging to the Association should be invited to compete'. His suggestion was met with favour, and the rules of the tournament were agreed three months later.

So, later that year, the inaugural FA Cup got under way with fifteen teams. The first-ever Cup goal was scored by Jarvis Kenrick of Clapham Rovers. The first final was played in 1872 at London's Kennington Oval, where 2,000 people paid a shilling each to see Wanderers (a team formed by ex-public school and university players) beat Royal Engineers 1-0. The first trophy, much smaller than the one in use today, was made by Martin, Hall & Co. at a cost of £20. Wanderers won the Cup three years in a row in the 1870s, and within the competition rules were entitled to keep it, but they decided to leave it with the FA on the condition that other teams would do the same. The trophy, which became popularly known as the 'Little Tin Idol', remained in use until 1895. Having been won by Aston Villa and put on display in a shop window in Birmingham, it was subsequently stolen, and despite a £10 reward it was never recovered.

The second Cup was a replica of the first and was used up until 1910, when the FA became aware that it had been pirated, so it was withdrawn and presented to Lord Kinnaird to mark his tenure of more than two decades as FA President. (It was recently sold at Christie's in 2005 for £478,400.) In 1911 the FA commissioned a company in Bradford to make the new, larger design still in use today. Weirdly, Bradford City won it in its first outing, and that remains the only time that a team from Bradford has ever reached the final.

After 80 years of hard usage, the Cup was replaced with an exact replica in 1991, and to this day it remains one of the most famous trophies in the world.

MOST MEMORABLE MOMENTS:

■ Wembley hosted its first final in 1923, having just been completed in under a year at a cost of £750,000. Although capacity for the new stadium was 127,000, it's thought that 200,000 spectators made it through the turnstiles before the gates were closed.

With thousands having to spill onto the pitch, the game was about to be abandoned (despite the presence of King George V in the Royal Box) when mounted police – and famously PC George Scorey on his white horse, Billy – slowly managed to push the crowds back to the sides of the field of play. Although the match got under way only 45 minutes late, it was then played in particularly peculiar circumstances. When a player stepped up to take a corner, he had to wait while police negotiated him a run-up through the crowd; and when one of the goals went in, it rebounded off the spectators behind the goal and back into play so quickly that few people realised a goal had been scored. When the ball went in for the other goal, one of the defenders was totally missing from his position because he was trapped in the crowd!

■ The 1938 Preston vs. Huddersfield final was the first to be televised live in full. The Cup's new audience was starting to wonder what all the fuss was about when, after nearly an hour and a half's football, there was still no score. Then, in the very last minute of extra time, Preston's George Mutch was up-ended in the box and his team awarded a penalty. In spite of still being badly dazed, Mutch stepped up and fired the spot-kick against the underside of the bar and into the goal.

■ Stanley Matthews had been a losing finalist for Blackpool in both 1948 and 1951 before reaching his third final for the team at 38 years of age in 1953. At 3-1 down against Bolton with 22 minutes left to play, he must have thought he had missed his last chance of a winner's medal. The tenacity and brilliance of Matthews ensured that this wasn't to be the case, however, helping drag his team back to level terms before his cross in the 90th minute set up Bill Perry to shoot home inside the near post for a 4-3 winner. It has since been dubbed 'The Matthews Final', which is a clear indication of his efforts when you think that his friend and team-mate Stan Mortensen scored a hat-trick in the match to draw the teams level.

Matthews later became the first player to be knighted for services to the game.

■ The 1956 final saw Manchester City take on Birmingham City. In goal for Man City that day was the German Bert Trautmann (who just over a decade before had been a British prisoner of war). About fifteen minutes from the end of the game he was forced to make a save at the lunging feet of Birmingham's Peter Murphy, and in the process he damaged his neck. In spite of the injury and the obvious pain, he played on and helped his side beat Birmingham 3-1 to secure the FA Cup.

An X-ray after the game revealed that he'd broken his neck.

■ In 1972, non-League Hereford took on the mighty First Division Newcastle United at St James's Park and amazingly secured a draw. This prompted Newcastle's Malcolm McDonald to promise that he would score ten in the replay at Hereford's tiny-by-comparison Edgar Street ground when they re-met. Well, he didn't manage ten, but he did put Newcastle 1-0 up eight minutes from time.

Then, with only four minutes left to play, Hereford's Ronnie Radford received the ball near the half-way line and started to run at the Newcastle goal. Looking somewhat dishevelled with his socks around his ankles, he proceeded to unleash a 30-yard missile into the top corner and, in the process, write himself into FA Cup folklore. His subsequent celebratory run, weaving across the pitch while chased by his own adoring fans, remains one of the tournament's most enduring moments. Radford's goal took the game to half an hour of extra time, in which Hereford's Ricky George slid home a close-range winner to complete one of the most famous bits of 'giant-killing' the Cup has ever seen.

■ In 1973, a Leeds side honed on the rigours of European club football and containing ten internationals went to the final as Cup-holders. It was their third FA Cup final in four years. They met Second Division Sunderland. No team from the Second Division had won the competition for more than 40 years and, as you might imagine, no one gave Sunderland a hope. To everyone's amazement, the underdogs went 1-0 up, but then followed the inevitable onslaught from the star-studded Leeds. Nevertheless, the Second Division side defended to within an inch of their lives, including one ridiculously impossible double save from Jim Montgomery to deny the brilliant Peter Lorimer. It's still regarded by many as the greatest save at Wembley, while some consider it the best save ever seen. Either way, it comprehensively wrote his name into Mackem folklore.

In spite of unrelenting raids from Leeds right to the final whistle, Sunderland desperately held on to win 1-0, producing one of the greatest upsets in the history of the Cup.

■ In the 1988 final, rank outsiders Wimbledon took on Liverpool in the final just eleven years after being elected into the Football League. Wimbledon, who had been in the Fourth Division only five years before, were priced at 33-1 before the third round in January, and Liverpool had just been crowned League Champions and were going for their second double in three seasons – they were the hottest favourites for years.

However, in the 37th minute – and very much against the run of play, which had included a disallowed Liverpool goal – Wimbledon's Lawrie Sanchez scored his first FA Cup goal to give the underdogs a 1-0 lead. That lead looked to be relatively short-lived when, in the 61st minute, Liverpool were awarded a penalty and John Aldridge stepped up to take it (having been successful with his previous eleven attempts from the spot). Dave Beasant, Wimbledon's 6'4" goalkeeper captain, then produced a brilliant save, turning the spot-kick round his left-hand post – the first-ever penalty save seen in a Wembley final. After holding on to this slim lead for the remainder of the game, Beasant also became the first goalkeeper to receive the Cup – on this occasion from HRH The Princess of Wales.

■ On Saturday 13 May 2006, with the new Wembley Stadium still not ready, Liverpool and West Ham met at the Millennium Stadium in Cardiff for what turned out to be one of the greatest finals the competition has ever seen.

Having come third in the Premiership, just behind a resurgent Man Utd and a rampant Chelsea, the Champions League holders Liverpool were clear favourites against a mid-table West Ham. But this was the FA Cup.

Twenty-eight minutes into the game, and a battling West Ham were already 2-0 up and looking to be on their way to a massive Cup upset. Liverpool had other ideas, however, and in the next 28 minutes of play scored two goals of their own through Djibril Cissé and Steven Gerrard to draw the scores level at 2-2. Ten minutes later, Alan Pardew's West Ham went ahead again when Paul Konchesky, seemingly attempting a deep cross to Marlon Harewood, looped the ball over José Reina and into the net to make it 3-2.

Then came the inevitable Liverpool pressure – another 28 minutes of it – until in the 91st minute, and with time almost up, Gerrard unleashed a 35-yard screamer into the left corner of the net to make it 3-3 and force the game to extra time.

The next half hour saw the

tiredness set in, with a succession of injuries as a result. West Ham had already made their three permitted substitutions during normal time, and consequently couldn't replace Harewood once he sustained a foot injury that ensured he could only limp around the pitch at the most important part of the game.

In the dying moments, West Ham won a free kick just outside the Liverpool box. Yossi Benayon floated the ball into the middle, which his 21-year-old captain Nigel Reo-Coker headed towards the far top corner of the net. Reina dived high into the air and produced a remarkable save, tipping the ball high on to the post. As the ball rebounded off the woodwork, it fell to Harewood's left foot – the one limb on the entire pitch that wasn't working properly – and consequently he sliced it wide. For the second time in succession (and only the second time it has ever happened), the FA Cup final went to penalties.

In the Champions League less than twelve months before, Liverpool had found themselves in exactly the same situation on that famous night in Istanbul, having come from behind to secure a 3-3 draw. It was an experience that was to stand them in good stead, as they went on to beat West Ham 3-1 in the penalty shoot-out, avert a major FA Cup upset, and secure the hallowed trophy for the seventh time.

IT'S BEEN WON THE MOST TIMES BY:

Manchester United – 11, followed by Arsenal's 10.

MOST APPEARANCES BY A TEAM IN AN FA CUP FINAL:

Manchester United and Arsenal – 17.

IT'S MADE OF:

Silver.

HEIGHT:

48.3 cm, excluding the plinth.

WEIGHT:

5,175 g.

BOOZE CAPACITY:

Enough to keep you arguing with your manager for a week.

MANTELPIECE KUDOS:

Phenomenal, and you'll get to keep it there, as your wife can change the ribbons to match the sofa.

ESSENTIAL FACTS:

■ The record score in an FA Cup match was set in 1887 when Preston North End beat Hyde United 26-0.

■ In 1889, Preston then became the first club to secure the League and Cup 'Double'. As if that wasn't impressive enough, they had won the league without suffering a single defeat (an achievement not repeated in the top flight until Arsenal did it in 2004). And as if *that* wasn't enough, they had also won the Cup without conceding a single goal. I don't think anyone begrudged them their nickname, the Invincibles.

■ Before becoming President of the FA, the Hon. Arthur Kinnaird appeared in no fewer than nine FA Cup finals when he played for Old Etonians and Wanderers in the 1870s and 80s. This is an achievement unmatched by any player in any era, and it saw him win twice with Old Etonians and three times with Wanderers (scoring in both the 1873 and 1878 finals).

■ In 1983, a year after becoming the youngest player in a World Cup, Norman Whiteside became the youngest player to score in an FA Cup final. The precocious Irishman was eighteen years and nineteen days old when he slotted home Man United's second in their 4-0 drubbing of Brighton and Hove Albion.

■ In 1986, Liverpool's Ian Rush scored twice as they beat Everton 3-1 in the first all-Merseyside final. Three years later, after a spell in Italy, he returned to slot another two against the same opposition. Then, against Sunderland in 1992, he scored his fifth goal in an FA Cup final; more than any other player.

Rush scored 43 FA Cup goals in the tournament as a whole throughout his career, second only to Henry Cursham of Notts County, who fired home 48 in a ten-year period from 1877 to 1887.

■ Curtis Weston is the FA Cup's youngest-ever finalist, coming on for Millwall as a substitute in their 3-0 loss to Man United in 2004 at the tender age of seventeen years and 119 days old. At the other end of the scale, the oldest player to grace a final is Walter 'Billy' Hampson, who, in 1924, at 41 years and 257 days old, helped Newcastle United beat Aston Villa 2-0.

■ In 1956, Leeds United were drawn at home to Cardiff City in the Third Round and lost 2-1.
   In 1957, Leeds United were drawn at home to Cardiff City in the Third Round and lost 2-1.
   In 1958, Leeds United were drawn at home to Cardiff City in the Third Round and lost 2-1.
   Weird.

■ The Cup had been going for twenty years before the penalty-kick was even invented.

■ There was an estimated TV audience of 10,000

for the first fully-televised final between Huddersfield Town and Preston North End in 1938. The Arsenal and Man Utd final in 2005 had an estimated audience of 484 million.

■ What do Charlton's Bert Turner (1946) and Manchester City's Tommy Hutchison (1981) have in common? They share the same dubious distinction of having scored for both sides in the same Cup final.

■ In 1970, while playing for Bournemouth, Scottish striker Ted MacDougall scored six goals in their First Round replay against Oxford City. Not satisfied with that, he notched up nine against Margate the following year, still a record for the Cup.

■ The Druids of Ruabon were the first Welsh club to compete in the competition, in 1877.

■ In the 1887–88 season, Preston North End's Scottish striker Jimmy Ross scored a phenomenal nineteen FA Cup goals. One hundred and twenty years later, this record remains intact.

■ The FA withhold a player's commemorative medal if they are sent off during a final.

■ What is always taken to the FA Cup final, but never used?

The losing team's ribbons.

■ Alvechurch and Oxford City had to play their 1971 Fourth Round tie six times before finding a winner. Nine goals were scored over eleven hours, making it the longest tie in the history of the FA Cup.

■ Referees receive £525 for officiating at the FA Cup final.

BEST KEPT:

In the sun on that bit of turf you weirdly bought and planted in your back garden when the old Wembley was taken down.

THE CLARET JUG

THE CLARET JUG

AWARDED FOR WINNING:

The Open Championship – golf's oldest major. Basically the most prestigious golf tournament in the world.

CONTESTED BY:

156 of the world's best golfers.

A BRIEF HISTORY:

When the Open Championship began in 1860, for the first ten years it was played solely at Prestwick and the winners were awarded with the Challenge Belt. Similar to those awarded in boxing, although considerably more sensibly sized, it was made of rich Moroccan leather and adorned with a silver buckle and emblems. However, a new trophy was required in 1870 after Young Tom Morris was allowed to keep the Belt for winning the Open three years in succession.

Suddenly the tournament no longer had a trophy to award and Prestwick didn't have the necessary cash to commission a new one. So the members at Prestwick came up with the idea of sharing the Open with the Royal and Ancient Golf Club (R&A) of St Andrews and the Honourable Company of Edinburgh Golfers, who at that time were based at Musselburgh's 9-hole Old Course. Prestwick suggested that the three clubs take it in turns to host the Open and also split the cost of the new trophy three ways.

After a couple of years of faffing about (in which they failed to organise an 1871 Open), they finally agreed on Prestwick's proposal on 11 September 1872, and commissioned the Golf Champion Trophy, or Claret Jug as it is now popularly known. Hallmarked 1873, it was made by Mackay Cunningham and Company of Edinburgh at a cost of £30, each club contributing £10.

As the 1872 event was organised at the last minute, the trophy wasn't ready in time to be presented to the winner Tom Morris, so Tom Kidd became the first winner to be actually presented with the Claret Jug after winning the Open in 1873 at St Andrews. It was then presented to the winner every year for almost half a century. Over that time, a number of other clubs entered the rota of hosts for the tournament, notably Muirfield in 1892 (the first championship contested away from the original three) and then Kent's Royal St George's in 1894 (when the championship left Scotland for the first time).

Three months after Bobby Jones won the championship at St Andrews in 1927, the Championship Committee of the R&A decided that 'in future the original Open Championship Cup be retained in possession of the R&A and that a duplicate be obtained for presentation to the winners'.

The original Claret Jug has been on permanent display at the clubhouse at St Andrews since 1928. The original Championship belt is also on display there, having been donated in 1908 by the Morris family.

The current Claret Jug was first awarded to Walter Hagen for winning the 1928 Open, and it is returned each year for presentation to the new champion, but many winners privately commission copies of the ancient jug for their own personal collections.

MOST MEMORABLE MOMENTS:

■ In the second round of the 1949 Open at Royal St George's, Sandwich, Harry Bradshaw's ball landed in a broken bottle at the 5th hole. Instead of waiting for a ruling, the Irishman decided to play the ball where it lay, and consequently shot a six.

Ultimately the decision was to cost Bradshaw dearly, as at the end of 72 holes he was tied with South Africa's Bobby Locke on 283. The Irishman lost the subsequent play-off by a huge twelve-stroke margin.

■ Following a head-on collision with a Greyhound bus in 1949, the great Ben Hogan did very little travelling. However, in 1953, his fellow American competitors Walter Hagen, Tommy Armour and Gene Sarazen persuaded him to compete outside America.

Hogan travelled to Carnoustie (having never competed with the new, smaller-sized golf ball before) and his aggregate 282 saw him lift the Claret Jug.

He never competed in the Open again.

■ Through his charismatic approach to the game, the legendary Arnold Palmer is largely credited with rekindling overseas interest in the Open and helping make it the Championship it is today. Royal Troon in 1962 played host to the 'King' as he successfully defended his Claret Jug. It witnessed Palmer destroy the field, cruising to a six-stroke win and posting a new Open record aggregate total of 276 in the process.

■ Argentinian Roberto de Vicenzo might be remembered most for his misfortune at the Masters when he mistakenly entered a 4 on his card for the 17th when actually he'd made a birdie 3. The mistake cost him a play-off place, prompting the famous quote: 'What a stupid I am!'

However, he should be remembered best for his Open Championship triumph in 1967. Having first competed for the Claret Jug in 1948, he came second once and third five times before finally becoming champion aged 44, beating the mighty Jack Nicklaus by two strokes.

■ St Andrews in 1970 saw the most famous miss in Open history. Having gone down the 18th needing just a par 4 to become Open Champion, American Doug Sanders missed a three-foot putt that would have seen him lift the Claret Jug. The miss forced him into an eighteen-hole play-off with fellow American Jack Nicklaus the following day, which Sanders then lost on the final hole.

Years later, asked if the putt still haunted him, he replied: 'No. Some days I can go twenty minutes without thinking about it.'

■ At Troon in 1973, 71-year-old Gene Sarazen competed some 50 years after his appearance at the course's inaugural Open in 1923. That didn't stop the 1932 Champion recording a hole-in-one at the infamous par-3 8th hole. He found the Postage Stamp with a five iron before watching his ball roll into the hole.

■ In 1974 at Royal Lytham and St Annes, Gary Player looked set for a relatively easy victory when things started to go a little wrong. First he pulled his second on the 17th into the deep rough; he found it only with the help of spectators, and with just seconds of the allotted time limit remaining. It was buried so deeply that he could only hack it on about five feet, and consequently he dropped a shot on the hole.

Then, on the 18th, he overshot his approach shot to the green. It finished up so close to the clubhouse wall that the right-handed South African had to hit it left-handed with the back of his putter. The ball landed on the green, ensuring that he secured the Claret Jug for the third time.

■ Having gone head-to-head at the Masters earlier in the year, Jack Nicklaus and Tom Watson again found themselves in a golfing showdown in the blisteringly hot 1977 Open at Turnberry.

In the first round, both players carded a two under par 68. In the second round, both players matched each other again, going round in par. In the third round, they both turned up the heat, again matching each other, but this time with a round of five under par. The scene was set for the conclusion of what has come to be known as the 'Duel in the Sun'.

They went down the 17th still level after four days of golf, but whereas Watson secured a birdie, Nicklaus missed a relatively short but downhill birdie putt, meaning he only got par.

Watson then crashed his drive right down the middle of the 18th, but again Nicklaus came unstuck as he pushed his tee shot into the rough, right next to some gorse. Watson then played his second, a beautiful seven-iron to within a few feet of the hole, apparently securing him the Claret Jug. Nicklaus had other ideas, though, and amazingly made it to the edge of the green from the deep rough with his second before holing out from more than 40 feet. All of a sudden what appeared like a done deal for Watson meant that he had only one putt for the Championship. Needless to say, the great man nailed it and won the showdown by a single stroke.

Nicklaus and Watson had finished ten and eleven shots clear of the field respectively, their 268 and 269 destroying the tournament record of 276. The 18th hole at Turnberry has since been renamed Duel in the Sun in recognition of this mighty golfing clash.

■ At Royal Lytham in 1979, 22-year-old Severiano Ballesteros entered the final day two shots off American Hale Irwin's lead. The young Spaniard battled hard, posting a 34 on the front nine before the defining moment of his round came at the short par-4 16th.

He stepped up on the tee with his first Open Championship in his sights, only to balloon his tee shot into a small car park about 50 yards to the right of the green. Fortunately for the Spaniard, the locked cars constituted immovable obstructions, and so he was allowed a free drop.

Ballesteros then hit his recovery shot to the edge of the green before dropping a 25-foot birdie putt. He was on his way to securing the Claret Jug for the first time.

■ On the final day at St Andrews in 1995, American John Daly seemingly had the tournament wrapped up. However, over the last few holes, Italy's Costantino Rocca made his charge for the Claret Jug, and the Open that year saw a thrilling climax.

On the par-4 16th, Rocca took three strokes whereas Daly took five, immediately clawing back two. Then, on the infamous Road Hole 17th, Daly dropped another shot. Rocca made a meal of it as well, his second shot landing on the road, bouncing onto the wall behind and back onto the road, finally coming to rest in a small hole. Despite the disastrous lie and having to putt from the road, the Italian remarkably got down in two to save par, leaving him just one stroke behind Daly going down the last.

On the 18th, and probably needing at least a birdie to force a play-off, Rocca hit his drive left and short of the green. Not a problem if he had managed to make it over the infamous Valley of Sin with his second, but the Italian fluffed his chip shot about five yards to leave himself about 60 feet from the pin.

That was it – surely the game was up? But not quite, as Rocca proceeded to sink the next, absurdly difficult birdie putt through the 18th's Valley of Sin to secure a play-off.

Rocca lying on his front and hammering the ground with his fists in a combination of celebration and relief remains one of the Open's most enduring images.

■ At Carnoustie in 1999, Paul Lawrie became the first Scotsman to win the Claret Jug since 1985, and the first to do so on native soil in 68 years. He was also the first player to win it having come through the pre-tournament local qualifying competition since the introduction of automatic entry for the world's best players in 1963. Most importantly, though, he had completed the greatest comeback in Open history, starting the final round ten strokes off the lead. Despite all this, the 1999 Open is probably more remembered for the way in which Jean Van de Velde threw the tournament away.

By the end of the third round, the Frenchman was five strokes ahead of the field – the record lead for an eventual non-winner in the history of the Championship. Although the gap had closed by the time he reached the last hole on the final day, he still needed only a double bogey 6 to secure the Claret Jug. Cue carnage.

Van de Velde took a driver and sliced his tee

shot into the rough. He then drilled a two-iron into the grandstand, ending up in even deeper rough just behind the hole's infamous Barry Burn. The rough was sufficient to catch his club face on the downswing of his third and the ball just plopped into the burn, prompting him to roll up his trousers and remove his shoes and socks before entering the water to consider playing the ball.

After much contemplation he decided against it and took a penalty drop, but then played his following shot into a greenside bunker. He then successfully played out of the bunker but left himself a seven-foot putt not to secure him victory, but for a triple bogey 7 and just to ensure that he made it into a three-way play-off with Lawrie and American Justin Leonard.

He made the putt but the rest, as they say, is history.

IT'S BEEN WON THE MOST TIMES BY:

Harry Vardon, with six victories. James Braid, J.H. Taylor, Peter Thomson and Tom Watson have all won it five times.

IT'S MADE OF:

Silver and wood.

PRIZE MONEY THAT COMES WITH IT:

In 1864, Old Tom Morris won the first Champion's cash prize of £6. By 2006, the winner's cheque had increased 120,000-fold to £720,000, or 2,000-fold if you allow for inflation.

MANTELPIECE KUDOS:

Your girlfriend's slightly disapproving parents are coming round for Sunday lunch. Decant the wine into it before serving. It could be anything, even vinegar. Her father will have you married off by tea.

CLEANING/MAINTENANCE REQUIRED:

A little spittle and a good buff with a member of the Royal and Ancient Championship Committee's old moth-eaten tweed pants.

ESSENTIAL FACTS:

■ When Tiger Woods won the Open Championship for the first time at St Andrews in 2000, he became only the fifth player in the history of the game to win all four majors, and the youngest ever to do so. He shot a 19 under par total of 269, the lowest score in relation to par ever recorded at a major. He finished eight shots ahead of anyone else – the largest winning margin at the event in 87 years.

Perhaps it had something to do with the fact that he didn't find a single one of the Old Course's 112 bunkers over the four days. Significantly, he beat by one shot Nick Faldo's record 18 under par 270 that he scored to win the Open at St Andrews in 1990, the difference being that Faldo hit one bunker that year.

■ Harry Vardon, J.H. Taylor and Gary Player have all won the Claret Jug in three different decades.

■ In the final round at Royal Lytham and St Annes in 2001, Ian Woosnam, who has never won the tournament, was tied for the lead until he incurred a two-stroke penalty as a result of his caddy having fifteen clubs in his bag instead of the regulatory maximum of fourteen.

Needless to say, he didn't win, the error also costing him £218,334 in prize money and a place in Europe's 2002 Ryder Cup team. The caddy somehow kept his job until a couple of weeks later, when he turned up late on the first tee after a night on the town. Woosnam lost patience and gave him the chop.

■ In the past, there was a table in the interview room at the Open each year that the press officer asked all past champions to sign. The story goes that when Colin Montgomerie came in for his pre-tournament interview one year, he saw the names on the table and grabbed a pen, only to be told he wasn't allowed.

■ In 1867, Old Tom Morris became the Open Championship's oldest-ever winner, aged 46 years and 99 days.

■ The following year his son, Young Tom Morris, became the Open's youngest-ever winner, aged seventeen years, five months and three days.

■ Young Tom Morris is also the Open's youngest-ever competitor, entering in 1865 at the tender age of fourteen years, four months and 25 days.

■ When Gene Sarazen played in the Open in 1976, he became the tournament's oldest-ever competitor, aged 74 years, four months and nine days.

■ On the tee of the monster 554-yard 16th hole at Hoylake in the first round of 2006, Tiger Woods pulled out his driver for the first time that Open Championship. He stepped up and spanked it — according to the R&A's new radar technology — at 191 miles an hour, and it came to rest 327 yards away in the middle of the fairway; the only problem being that it was the wrong fairway. Nevertheless, Woods still made birdie.

In spite of his recovery, it was the only time in the entire tournament that he got his driver out of his bag. Even so, it didn't stop the American from picking up fourteen shots of his 18 under par final score on the par 5s and romping home to his eleventh major title.

■ Nine courses make up the current rota of hosts for the Open Championship. They are as follows:

Carnoustie
Muirfield
Royal Birkdale
Royal Liverpool
Royal Lytham and St Annes
Royal St George's
Royal Troon
St Andrews
Turnberry

■ A further five courses have hosted the Open in the past but are no longer in the rota:

Musselburgh
Prestwick
Prince's
Royal Cinque Ports
Royal Portrush

■ When Greg Norman won the Claret Jug at Royal St George's in 1993, he went 66, 68, 69, 64 to finish on 267, still the lowest aggregate score in the tournament's history.

■ Frank Stranahan shot a round of 66 at Royal Troon in 1950. So did Tiger Woods at Royal Lytham in 1996, then so did Justin Rose at Royal Birkdale two years after that. Not bad, considering they were all amateurs at the time.

In fact, Woods' round contributed to his 281 that year – the lowest aggregate score by an amateur in the history of the Open.

■ It took England's Denis Durnian just 28 shots to get round the front nine of Royal Birkdale in 1983. This remains a record for any nine holes of golf – front, middle, or back – in Open history.

■ At Muirfield in 2002, Colin Montgomerie shot a brilliant second-round 7 under par 64. The following day he hacked his way round for 84, equalling a record set way back in 1938 by R.G. French for the most significant variation in score between two rounds.

■ Tiger Woods' Dad used to test his son's concentration by jingling change around in his pocket while he was putting.

■ At a monstrous 7,361 yards, Carnoustie in 1999 was the longest course in Open history.

■ Jack Nicklaus has recorded more rounds under par in pursuit of the Claret Jug than any other player, shooting 61 of the beauties down the years before his retirement in 2005.

■ When American Tom Weiskopf won at Troon in 1973, he took the lead in the first round and never relinquished it, finishing with a total of 276, three strokes clear of the rest of the field.

■ There has never been a Welsh champion.

■ The Claret Jug has appeared on two different Scottish £5 notes – first in 2004 to commemorate the 250th anniversary of the Royal and Ancient Golf Club, and then in 2005, when a picture of Jack Nicklaus holding the trophy that he won three times in his career was used to mark the retirement of the great man.

■ The engraver sometimes starts work on the trophy before it's a done deal. No egg on face as yet ...

BEST KEPT:

Next to the cheese.

THE WIMBLEDON
GENTLEMEN'S SINGLES
CHAMPIONSHIP TROPHY

THE WIMBLEDON MEN'S SINGLES CHAMPIONSHIP TROPHY

AWARDED FOR WINNING:

The oldest and most prestigious tennis tournament in the world, the only Grand Slam event with a very strict dress code and, more importantly, the only one played on grass.

CONTESTED BY:

128 of the world's best tennis players based on international rankings or success in the qualifying tournament held the week before, although the committee can admit a player without a high enough ranking as a *wildcard*.

A BRIEF HISTORY:

Founded in 1868 as The All England Croquet Club, it was only when the committee realised the popularity of tennis that they made some space for a couple of courts in the club's facilities and called it The All England Tennis and Croquet Club. Back on track then by 1877, they advertised a 'lawn tennis meeting, open to all amateurs, entrance fee £1 1s 0d', in the weekly sporting magazine *The Field*, and said that entrants should bring their own rackets and 'shoes without heels', although balls would be supplied by the club gardener.

So, with the exciting prospect of paying to wear their own shoes, 22 competitors entered, and in typically grim British weather they contested the inaugural Wimbledon Men's Singles Trophy in front of a temporary stand made of planks of wood that offered seating for 30 people. It also turned out that the winner, 27-year-old Spencer

Gore, was more interested in cricket than tennis.

In spite of its somewhat lacklustre begin-nings, it has become what is widely regarded, by players and pundits alike, as the greatest tennis championship in the world today. Not without a few issues along the way, however – notably in 1968, when, as a result of the 'living lie' of amateurism or 'shamateurism' as it was otherwise known, the tournament had to turn professional, ushering in the open era. Although this passed off smoothly enough, everything got a little more serious for a while and in 1973, 79 players – including thirteen of the sixteen seeds – went on strike and withdrew from the tournament in a silly dispute over who was in charge of world tennis as a whole. The decision by Bjorn Borg not to withdraw and the first manifestation of 'Borgmania' (thousands of screaming teenage girls diving around and fainting wherever he went) helped see the tournament through a troubled year. Other than these minor blips and the inevitable annual farce that is British weather, the Championship has continued to be the most prestigious in the world, and the gilt silver trophy is still the one that all tennis players want to get their hands on. In use since the very first

Wimbledon back in 1877, it is inscribed 'The All England Lawn Tennis Club Single Handed Champion of the World', which does throw up the argument that all these men in the modern era who win it using a double-handed backhand should be presented with an inferior plastic version as punishment for behaving like a big girl.

MOST MEMORABLE MOMENTS:

■ In 1974, Australian Ken Rosewall, aged 39, reached the final for a fourth time, some twenty years after his first.

■ 1980 saw a monster of a Borg and McEnroe final. Although a five-set classic, it will be specifically remembered for the absurdly long tie-break in the fourth set. With some of the best tennis Centre Court had ever seen, it comprised 34 points (a record for a Wimbledon final), lasted more than 22 minutes and saw McEnroe save five championship points before finally winning the set and sending it to a fifth. This also turned out to be a bit of an epic, Borg finally winning 8-6 on his eighth match point, giving him his fifth title in succession – equalling a record set by Britain's William Renshaw way back in the 1880s.

■ In the first match on his way to the 1981 title, McEnroe was warned by the umpire for smashing up his racket. 'Man, you can not be serious!' was his response, before demanding to see, and then unleashing on, the tournament referee: 'You guys are the absolute pits of the world, do you know that?' Genteel Wimbledon had never seen any-thing like it.

■ In 1984, an unknown German boy by the name of Boris Becker made his first appearance at Wimbledon. During his third round match he fell awkwardly on his ankle and had to be carried from the court. The injury was sufficient to ensure that he didn't go near another tennis court for more than three months.

The following year, fully recovered, yet still only seventeen, unseeded and still relatively unknown, Becker returned to SW19. He faced the seventh seed Joakim Nystrom in the second round, and the game looked to be up early for the German when the Swede found himself serving for the match. In spite of this, Becker came through, winning 9-7 in a marathon fifth set.

The next round wasn't much easier. Becker twisted his ankle in the third set and considered retiring from the tournament, until some emergency courtside treatment enabled him to continue. He eventually beat Tim Mayotte, but not before the American had been two sets to one ahead and held two match points in the fourth set. Despite his injury, Becker saved the match points and fought back to win in five sets.

He then played four sets in his quarter-final against Frenchman Henri Leconte, and in the semi-final needed another four sets to get past Sweden's Anders Jarryd. In the final he met the American Kevin Curren, who had duly despatched both the number one seed John McEnroe and double former champion Jimmy Connors on his route through the draw. In spite of this, Becker was too good, again winning in four sets and establishing a collection of new records.

He had played a staggering 292 games. Of his seven matches, four of them had gone to four sets and twice he had faced five. In doing so, he had dropped eight sets on his way to the Championship, equalling the record set by the American Ted Schroeder in 1949. More importantly, he became the first German champion, was the first unseeded champion, and at seventeen years and 227 days, was also the youngest-ever champion of Wimbledon and, at that time, any Grand Slam event (Michael Chang won the French Open in 1989 aged seventeen years and three months).

■ 'Pistol' Pete Sampras arrived to defend his title in 2000 having lost only one match at Wimbledon in the last seven years. By now, this success looked unlikely to continue, given his age and the back injury he was carrying. To make matters worse, he picked up acute tendinitis in his left shin in the second round, leaving him unable to train between matches. In spite of all this, he dropped only two sets getting to the final, in which he met Australian Pat Rafter.

Delayed by rain and having gone a set down, Sampras eventually won almost in the dark at just before 9 pm. He burst into tears before running to his parents at the back of the stands for a big hug. Not very macho, perhaps, but understandable given that not only had he just won Wimbledon for the seventh time (equalling Willie Renshaw's record set way back in 1889), but he had also won his thirteenth Grand Slam title, surpassing Roy Emerson's record tally of twelve.

■ Big-serving Croat Goran Ivanisevic's career was dogged by self-confessed multiple personalities. By his own admission, these were 'good Goran', 'bad Goran' and 'emergency Goran'. On one occasion 'bad Goran' ensured that he had to withdraw from a match in Brighton, having angrily broken all his available rackets.

And so in 2001, when ranked 125 in the world, he just made it into Wimbledon as a wildcard. Although carrying a shoulder injury and also giving his digestive system a bit of a shoeing by weirdly eating the same meal at the same table of the same restaurant for a fortnight, he managed to make it to his fourth Wimbledon final. Having lost his previous three, he finally managed to clinch the title when he beat Pat Rafter in a marathon five-setter on the tournament's third Monday. 'Emergency Goran' had prevailed, making him the only wildcard entrant to ever win the tournament. So excited was he by his victory, that on his return to his home town in Croatia, he did a striptease in front of more than 100,000 adoring fans.

MOST PAINFUL MOMENT:

Cliff Richard's impromptu rendition of 'Singing in the Rain' on Centre Court.

IT'S BEEN WON THE MOST TIMES BY:

William Renshaw (GB) and Pete Sampras (USA) – 7.

IT'S MADE OF:

Gilt silver.

HEIGHT:

47 cm.

WIDTH:

19 cm.

PRIZE MONEY THAT COMES WITH IT:

When prize money was first awarded in 1968, Australian champion Rod Laver received just £2,000. In 2006, Roger Federer received a rather better £655,000.

MANTELPIECE KUDOS:

Pretty damn cool unless you're a goth, in which case your goth mates will know you've had to dress all in white to win it and will probably not invite you to their next apple bobbing party.

ESSENTIAL FACTS:

■ Just under 10 per cent of the world's population is left-handed. However, the percentage of professional left-handed tennis players is lower, and the percentage of left-handed winners of Wimbledon, lower still.

The tournament had been going for 30 years before Australian Norman Brookes became the first left-hander to lift the trophy. As it happens, he was the first overseas champion as well.

It wasn't until Jaroslav Drobny, another 40 years later, that Wimbledon saw its next left-handed champion. Drobny, who had represented Croatia at ice hockey at the 1948 Winter Olympics, had chosen to flee his homeland's communist regime and was competing under an Egyptian passport when he won Wimbledon at 32 years old, on his eleventh attempt.

The bespectacled Drobny had reached the semi-finals three times and been runner-up twice before finally getting his hands on the trophy in 1954. A decade of dogged tenacity had endeared him enormously to the British public, who treated his four-set, 58-game classic victory in the final over Australian Ken Rosewall as pretty much a home win.

Drobny became a British citizen five years later.

■ From 1878 to 1921 the holder of the men's singles title would effectively get a bye to the final, not playing a solitary game until the Challenge Round, when he would play the winner of that year's tournament to decide the Championship.

■ In 1879, the younger son of an Irish baron by the name of Vere Thomas St Leger Goold became Irish tennis champion. Ebullient from his success, he set off to London to see if he could conquer Wimbledon as well. As a player who looked to attack at the net, his flamboyant play was a hit with the crowds, who were accustomed to the more gentle baseline game of the time. His increasingly large group of new-found fans watched him progress through the draw as he notched up victories against F. Durrant, J. Vans Agnew, A.J. Mulholland and G.E. Tabor to make the last four in the All-Comers Draw. He then received a bye but lost in the All-Comers Final, which, had he won, would have seen him challenge for the Championship.

On 6 August 1907, the following story appeared in *The Times*:

> After the arrival of the 5.38 train from Monte Carlo this morning, a man and a woman deposited a trunk and a handbag in the cloakroom. Shortly afterwards they asked the porter to send on the luggage to London. The porter, noticing a smell, informed the special police commissary of the station, who seized the two trunks. When opened they were found to contain the remains of a woman cut to pieces. The two travellers were immediately arrested.
>
> When interrogated by the examining magistrates, the prisoners said that they were husband and wife. They came from Monte Carlo. They denied having murdered the woman. According to their story, they only knew her through having met occasionally in the gaming rooms at Monte Carlo. On Sunday last she came to see them to ask for money ...

The accused couple claimed that while the woman was trying to borrow money from them, her lover had burst into the room and killed her. They went on to offer in their statement that – having been innocent witnesses to the crime – they didn't want to be implicated themselves and so had cut the woman into pieces in order to get rid of the evidence. The court case that followed helped establish the facts.

The two had got married in 1891 and shortly afterwards had emigrated to Canada. In 1903 they had returned to England to settle in Liverpool. They started a laundry business but it failed, so they moved to Monaco to try to get rich on the gaming tables. Inevitably, they fell further into debt and so had to borrow heavily. A Danish woman who had lent them a substantial sum came to their flat to ask for it back. A vicious argument ensued before the couple killed and brutally dismembered her.

The couple were found guilty and both sentenced to life imprisonment. She was sent to prison in Montpellier, where she died six years later, in 1914. He was taken to Devil's Island, the horrific French penal colony off

the South American coast. Vere Thomas St Leger
Goold lasted less than a year, before he died
aged 55.

And to think he was almost Wimbledon
champion.

■ For security reasons, the guest list for the
Royal Box is released only on the day. Previously,
players had to bow or curtsy to any members of
the Royal Family upon entering or leaving Centre
Court. In 2003, however, the President of the All
England Club, HRH The Duke of Kent, relaxed
the rules so that the formality is now required
only if either the Queen or the Prince of Wales
is present.

■ From 1949, all champions have received a
21.6 cm tall replica of the trophy to keep.

■ 1991 saw the wettest first week ever. After four
days, only 52 of the scheduled 240 matches had
been completed.

■ Court Number Two is known as the 'Graveyard
of Champions' due to its amusingly regular habit

of hosting the demise of top seeds in the first round.

■ Each year, just before the main event, a Wimbledon qualifying competition is held at the Bank of England Sports Club in Roehampton for those without the necessary world ranking to gain automatic acceptance into the main draw. Although for most qualifiers reaching the main tournament is achievement enough in itself, and they usually go out in the preliminary rounds, some others have fared rather better.

In 1977 an unknown eighteen-year-old called John McEnroe successfully negotiated his way through the qualifying tournament before going on to the semi-finals in the main draw, only to be beaten by top-seed Jimmy Connors in four sets.

More recently, in 2000, qualifier Vladimir Voltchkov of Belarus also reached the semi-finals, only to be beaten by the eventual champion, Pete Sampras.

■ A wooden racket was last used at Wimbledon in 1987.

■ There used to be a break of four days between the men's semi-final and the final to allow for the Eton vs. Harrow school cricket match at Lord's; difficult to believe, but true.

■ As he emerged as one of the new stars of tennis, Andre Agassi chose not to play at Wimbledon from 1988 to 1990, supposedly because of its stuffy traditionalism and in particular the 'Players must play predominantly in white' dress code which was introduced in 1963. People at the time rather suspected, however, that Agassi was avoiding the tournament because his predominantly baseline game wouldn't be suited to grass.

He then entered in 1991, which led to weeks of speculation by the press as to what he would wear when he turned up at SW19. He eventually came out for the first round in an entirely white outfit and went on to reach the quarter-finals.

■ In 1937 the American J.D. Budge somewhat greedily won not only the Gentlemen's Singles, but also the Doubles and the Mixed Doubles as well. Not content with that, he won all three again the following year.

■ In 1909 Britain's Arthur Gore became the event's oldest-ever champion, at 41 years and 182 days. In 1926 Britain's M.J.G. Ritchie became the oldest-ever competitor, at 55 years and 247 days. The following year, the event saw its youngest-ever entrant – America's S.B.B. Wood, at just fifteen years and 231 days.

■ In 2003 Croatia's 6'10" Ivo Karlovic became the tallest player ever to compete in the Men's Singles at Wimbledon. In fact, it was his first-ever Grand Slam tournament and he caused a major upset by beating defending champion Lleyton Hewitt in the first round.

Karlovic also has the record for the most aces served in a match. In 2005, he aced Italian Daniele Bracciali 51 times in their first-round match but still somehow managed to lose.

■ The shortest player ever to compete is the Philippines' Felicisimo Ampon. He played from 1948 to 1953 and was a pint-sized 4'11".

■ The club and its premises were used for a number of different purposes during the Second World War, including the farming of chickens and pigs. In October 1940, a stick of 500-lb bombs landed on Centre Court, destroying more than 1,200 seats.

■ It's thought that tennis's peculiar scoring system comes from the placement of a clock on early courts at the end of the 19th century. When a player won a point, the hand was moved first to 15 minutes past, then 30 minutes and so on. In time, 45 was shortened to 40, as it had fewer syllables and was quicker and easier to say.

■ Approximately 28,000 kg of strawberries and 7,000 litres of cream are consumed at the Championships each year.

BEST KEPT:

Next to your Cliff Richard commemorative plate.

THE OLYMPIC MEN'S
100m GOLD MEDAL

THE OLYMPIC MEN'S 100m GOLD MEDAL

AWARDED FOR WINNING:

The most anticipated and prestigious sprint race in the world.

CONTESTED BY:

After heats, the world's eight fastest men.

A BRIEF HISTORY:

The Games of the Olympiad began in 776 BC with lots of naked Greek men wrestling while covered in oil, and were held in Olympia, Greece for nearly 1,000 years. They gradually declined in importance as the Romans took hold of Greece, until Emperor Theodosius I – thinking it to be a pagan festival – banned them in 393 AD.

In 1896 a French nobleman by the name of Pierre de Coubertin revived the tradition, and the Athens Games of that year saw 43 events contested by only 245 competitors from fourteen nations (over 200 entrants were Greek). Nevertheless, no international sporting event of this magnitude had ever been organised before.

Bar the intervention of the two world wars, the Olympics have been held every four years since, and have grown to the 301 events of the 2004 Athens Games, which were contested by 11,099 athletes from 202 countries.

Despite the considerable change in events over the years, the 100-metre dash has been in place since day one of the modern era. Winners have not always received the gold medal, however. In 1896, winners' medals were in fact silver as, strangely, gold was considered an inferior metal at the time. The custom of gold-silver-bronze for the first three places did not come in until 1904, and has since been copied for many other sporting events across the world.

From 1928 to 1968, the same design by Florentine artist Giuseppe Cassioli was used (but with a differing name for the host city) on one side, and a generic design of an Olympic champion on the other. From 1972 to 2000 Cassioli's side remained, but a custom side by the host city was introduced at each Olympics on the other. Upon realising that Cassioli's design incorporated a Roman amphitheatre – for an institution that was born in Greece – a new design was commissioned for the Athens Olympics in 2004.

Originally the gold medals were solid gold. Don't tell anyone (certainly not Carl Lewis, who's got nine of them), but since 1912 they have been made of gilt silver. In spite of this, they are every world-class athlete's holy grail, and if you win one for the 100 metres, you can lay claim to being the fastest man on the planet.

MOST MEMORABLE MOMENTS:

■ The 1936 Olympics – or 'Hitler Olympics' as they are sometimes referred to – were held in the German capital, Berlin. With the Nazi doctrine already very clear, it was meant to be Hitler's showcase of Aryan superiority.

Instead, it was the year when African American Jesse Owens won four gold medals (100m, 200m, long jump and 4x100m relay), setting a new Olympic record in all but one of the four events. By the end, even the 100,000 partisan Germans in the Olympic Stadium were cheering his achievements.

As galling as his brilliance was for the Nazis, it is a common misconception that Owens was treated badly while competing in Germany, the sad reality being that he was afforded much more equality during his stay than he would have received back home. Segregation in the US was commonplace at that time, with black people denied the use of the same hotels, restaurants and transport as whites, none of which he encountered while in Germany.

It is also thought that Adolf Hitler snubbed Owens, but this isn't true either. On the first day of the Games, Hitler shook hands with just the German medal winners, but the Olympic Committee, unimpressed with his lack of neutrality, insisted he would have to congratulate everyone or no one. Hitler chose the latter, and didn't feature in any further medal presentations.

'When I came back to my native country, after all the stories about Hitler, I couldn't ride in the front of a bus', Owens said. 'I had to go to the back door. I couldn't live where I wanted. I wasn't invited to shake hands with Hitler, but I wasn't invited to the White House to shake hands with the President, either.'

A reception was organised for him at the Waldorf Astoria in New York, but he had to use the goods lift to get to it.

■ At the age of fourteen, American kid Lindy Remigino was bored and entered a 40-yard dash at the YMCA in his home town of Hartford, Connecticut. He won it easily and so decided to take up track and field at his high school. Seven years later he was Olympic champion.

Just prior to the 1952 Olympics, Remigino was certainly not considered among the world's best sprinters. He was not even among America's best sprinters. In fact, he had only just been ranked third in his college sprint team! It was only through the sickness of his school's top sprinter, then the injury of his compatriot Jim Golliday, and then the decision by another American, Andy Stanfield, to enter only the 200m, that Remigino found himself on the boat to Helsinki to compete in what was ultimately the most exciting 100m the Olympics had ever seen.

After the gun, Australia's John Treloar went into an early lead, but by the half-way mark the entire rest of the field, bar Jamaica's Herb McKenley, had drawn level. Over the next 30 metres Remigino powered into the lead, but behind him McKenley had caught and edged just ahead of the pack. In the meantime, Trinidad-born McDonald Bailey of

Britain had also entered the mix. Approaching the tape, Remigino pitched forward into a lean, causing him to slow, his deceleration sufficient to ensure that McKenley crossed the line at the same time. There was immediate confusion, as no one knew who had won. Remigino congratulated McKenley, as he was convinced that his premature dip for the line had allowed the Jamaican to beat him.

Eventually, having studied the photo, the officials decided that Remigino's shoulder had crossed the line less than an inch ahead of McKenley, and so they awarded him the gold medal. In fact, the race turned out to be so close that fourteen inches ultimately separated first and fourth place.

■ Robert Lee 'Bullet Bob' Hayes won the gold medal at the 1964 Tokyo Olympics, equalling the world record in the process. He then won another gold medal in the 4x100m relay, securing another world record in that as well. This was to be his last-ever race, however, as he immediately retired. Athletics' loss certainly turned out to be American football's gain, because by the end of the same year he had signed to the Dallas

Cowboys as a wide receiver – and in both of his first two seasons he was leading touchdown receiver. Opposing teams were forced to pioneer a new kind of zone defence whereby defenders would cover an area rather than an individual, as no single player could keep up with him.

A hugely successful career in the game culminated in him winning the Super Bowl in 1971, making him the only person ever to have won both a Super Bowl ring and an Olympic gold medal.

■ African American athlete Jim Hines went to the 1968 Olympics in Mexico having just become the first man in a 100m race to break the ten-second barrier. The black members of the US team were threatening to boycott the Games because of the inclusion of apartheid South Africa and the recent revelations linking the head of the International Olympic Committee with a racist and anti-Semitic country club. So although Hines nearly didn't run, he did, reached the final, and won it in a new world record time of 9.95 seconds – a record that was to remain intact for fifteen years.

■ 1972 will unfortunately forever be remembered for the Munich massacre. Eleven members of the Israeli team were taken hostage by eight Palestinian terrorists in the athletes' Olympic village. Two were killed before a failed rescue attempt left the other nine competitors, five terrorists and a policeman also dead.

■ During the athletics season of 1975, Hasely Joachim Crawford entered himself for only a handful of races in order to prepare for the Montreal Olympics the following year. The tactic worked, and he became 100m champion, winning Trinidad and Tobago's first-ever gold medal and assuring him the status of a demi-god back home. He has since appeared on stamps and has a national aeroplane and sports stadium named after him.

■ Initially a long jumper and a triple jumper, Scotsman Alan Wipper Wells started to take sprinting seriously in the 1970s. He never used starting blocks, although a rule change forced him to begin doing so at the 1980 Moscow Olympics. It didn't seem to bother him particularly, as he left with the 100m gold medal.

■ At the Los Angeles Games in 1984, Carl Lewis, whom many regard as the greatest athlete of all time, equalled Jesse Owens' achievement of four gold medals in the 100m, 200m, long jump and 4x100m. At his father's funeral in 1987, the Olympic champion pulled his Los Angeles 100-metre gold medal from his pocket and placed it in his dead father's hands. 'I want you to have this', he was heard to say, 'it was your favourite event.' When his mother expressed her surprise, he responded calmly: 'Don't worry, I'll get another one.'

■ Seoul, 24 September 1988, saw the most famous 100 metres ever run. No race, of any distance, has ever been so eagerly anticipated across the world. Canada's

Ben Johnson and American Carl Lewis had demonstrated in the years leading up to the Games that they were clearly the fastest two men on the planet, but it was now time to decide who was truly king. Lewis had been faster in the heats, Johnson going through only as fastest loser from the second round.

That was all about to change. As the gun went, Johnson fired out of his blocks and never looked back. Lewis got his characteristically slower start, but rather than overtaking his adversary, he had to look desperately to his right three times – only to find Johnson in front on each occasion. Johnson led for the entire race and hit a top speed of 43.4 km/h. He was so sure of victory that even before the end of the race he had pointed his index finger to the sky to indicate that he was the world's number one. He covered the 100m in just 46 strides before crossing the line at 9.79 seconds, destroying his own world record of 9.83 and, in the process, underlining his ascension to Lewis's throne. It's worth putting Johnson's time in context: from 1968 until 1983, the world record for the 100 metres had been improved by 0.04 seconds; in just one year, Johnson had slashed 0.16 seconds from it. Even in defeat, Lewis had set a new American record of 9.92 seconds.

Later, discussing the inevitable difference to his time made by his gesture of victory during the race, Johnson said: 'If I had gone through I would have got 9.75 – but I'm saving that for next year. Anyone can set a world record, but the gold medal is mine.'

■ The day after Johnson won his gold medal, while the whole planet was going mad for him and his phenomenal new world record, his urine sample was quietly being tested at an International Olympic Committee-accredited laboratory in Seoul. Stanozolol, an anabolic steroid, was found. Samples are deliberately unnamed so as to keep the athlete's identity a secret from the people working on it. It simply had a code on the bottle, which was then passed on to the chairman of the IOC medical commission, Prince Alexandre de Merode.

The Prince was staying at the Shilla Hotel in the centre of the city, with armed guards in sentry boxes placed around the perimeter of its hilly grounds. In his room, there was a safe in which lived the document that listed which code number corresponded with which athlete. And so, sitting alone at his hotel desk, the Prince was the first to know of Johnson's fate.

Johnson was woken in the night and told that the IOC had decided to send him home. He was stripped of his Olympic gold medal (which was given to Carl Lewis instead), his world record was declared null and void, and he was banned from competing for two years. He returned to Canada in disgrace.

■ 1996 was a peculiar race. In spite of it taking longer than any other Olympic final to get under way, it was also the fastest race ever run (well, if you don't count Johnson's disqualified effort in 1988). It began with three false starts, two of which were enough to disqualify the 36-year-old Linford Christie (the Olympic champion from 1992). Christie appealed, and so everyone had to wait for an official response from the Olympic stewards. The result finally came back – and it wasn't good news for Christie, who had to spend the race shaking his head on the sidelines.

When the race finally got under way, the eventual winner – Canadian Donavan Bailey – was slow out of his blocks. He was near the back of the field for some time, but by 60 metres he had reached a speed of 12.1 metres per second, charging past the rest. He crossed the line in 9.84 seconds (a new world record), followed by Namibia's Frank Fredericks in 9.89 and Ato Boldon of Trinidad and Tobago in 9.9 seconds. All three times were the fastest the Olympics had ever seen (again, if you don't count that naughty Ben Johnson).

IT'S BEEN WON THE MOST TIMES BY:

Carl Lewis (1984 and 1988).

ALLOY/COMPOUND:

It's a bit of a con really, because it's at least 92.5 per cent silver, gilded with just 6 grams of gold.

CLEANING/MAINTENANCE REQUIRED:

Nothing abrasive, or before you know it your medal will have turned silver and everyone will think you came second.

ESSENTIAL FACTS:

■ The relay of the Olympic flame was introduced at the Berlin Games in 1936. Despite being part of the premeditated self-glorification of the Third Reich, the tradition remains to this day. However, 2004 saw the ante upped somewhat with the first relay of the flame around the globe. It lasted 78 days and visited all previous Olympic cities, as well as Africa and Latin America for the first time. No fewer than 11,300 different torch-bearers covered the 78,000 km journey before the flame finally returned to Athens for the start of the Games.

■ 1920 saw the first Games after the end of the Great War. As a symbol of the world's new-found peace, it was decided that the release of doves would immediately follow the lighting of the Olympic flame. This tradition was very popularly received and it lasted for 68 years until 1988, when a number of the beautiful white birds were burned alive.

■ The majority of sprinters cover the 100 metres without taking a single breath.

■ Jesse Owens won his four gold medals in Berlin in 1936 wearing shoes made by a German manufacturer called Gebrüder Dassler Schuhfabrik. The company later split, becoming Adidas and Puma.

■ London will play host to the 2012 Olympics, making it the first city to hold the Games three times.

■ Ben Johnson was so slow when he first started sprinting as a young man that one member of his local team quit on the grounds that 'even Ben is beating me'.

■ The five interlinked Olympic rings represent the unity of the five continents at the event. The black, blue, green, red and yellow of the rings were chosen so that each nation in the world had at least one of them in their national flag.

■ Sixty-six nations including Canada, Japan, West Germany and the United States boycotted the 1980 Moscow Games following the Soviet invasion of Afghanistan. Notably, Australia, Great Britain and Greece didn't withdraw, making them the only three nations to have competed in every Summer Olympics in the modern era.

■ Ten more countries currently participate in the Summer Olympics than there are UN member states.

■ Reggie Edgar Walker achieved Olympic 100m gold when he was nineteen years and 128 days old. Although this was way back in 1908, he is still its youngest winner.

■ At the Olympics in 2000, Sydney had to find room for over 16,000 broadcasters and journalists, who helped ensure that the Games were watched by 3.8 billion people on television.

■ The time between the starter's gun and the first push against the starting block by a sprinter is measured electronically by sensors built into both the blocks and the gun. Scientists have established that the time it takes for the bang of the gun to reach the sprinters' ears, then for the human brain to process the sound and react to it, amounts to 0.1 seconds. Anything less is deemed a false start.

■ Previously a sprinter was disqualified only if responsible for two false starts in a race. At the beginning of 2003, however, the rule was changed so that after just one false start, anyone responsible for a subsequent jump of the gun would be immediately disqualified. This has led to mind games in which slower sprinters will deliberately use up the false start 'grace' so that from then on, with so much to lose, the favourites will be cautiously slow out of the blocks so as not to run the risk of being disqualified.

■ Ben Johnson won the 100m at the 1987 World Championships in Rome in a time of 9.83 seconds. Johnson was then interviewed after his victory, and it went something like this:

INTERVIEWER: 'Ben Johnson, you said you'd run 9.83 seconds and you ran 9.83 seconds! How do you explain that?'
BEN JOHNSON: 'I don't talk shit.'

He was live to more than 10 million viewers.

BEST KEPT:

Clean.

THE WILLIAM
WEBB ELLIS CUP

THE WILLIAM WEBB ELLIS CUP

AWARDED FOR WINNING:

The Rugby World Cup.

CONTESTED BY:

After qualifying, twenty of the world's best rugby-playing nations.

A BRIEF HISTORY:

It's widely believed that the game we know today was born in 1823 when a sixteen-year-old pupil of Rugby School, one William Webb Ellis, 'with a fine disregard for the rules of football as played in his time, first took the ball in his arms and ran with it, thus originating the distinctive feature of the Rugby game'. Sceptical as historians are of this view inscribed on a plaque at Rugby School, there's obviously something in it, as he's since had

Ellis Park in Johannesburg – a major international rugby union stadium – named after him. More importantly, he's also been immortalised in the Holy Grail of the rugby world – the Webb Ellis Trophy for which all rugby-playing nations compete in the quadrennial Rugby World Cup.

The actual cup is quite a bit older than the tournament it's contested for. It was chosen in February 1987 for the inaugural tournament of the same year, but the trophy itself was made by the crown jewellers, Garrard and Co., way back in 1906.

The notion of a Rugby World Cup had first been considered in 1979, but it wasn't until 1985 that its inception was finally agreed upon for 1987 – thereby avoiding a clash with the FIFA World Cup and the Olympics. A vote between the eight IRFB members of Australia, England, France, Ireland, New Zealand, Scotland, South Africa and Wales had established the tournament with six to two in favour. Ireland and Scotland had voted against, worried that it threatened the amateur status of the sport, and France's vote was dependent on countries outside the IRFB being invited to participate. South Africa was to be excluded due to apartheid, but voted in favour nonetheless. It left only two years to get the tournament ready, Argentina being invited to replace South Africa, and with further invitations extended to Zimbabwe, Canada, Fiji, Japan, Italy, Romania, Tonga and the United States.

The opening match saw the hosts, New Zealand, give Italy a mildly embarrassing 70-6 kicking, but other than the Italians, no one was worrying. Not only had it reunited a country divided by the rebel 'Cavaliers' tour of almost all of New Zealand's leading stars to apartheid South Africa the previous year, it had heralded the beginning of one of the world's greatest sporting events.

MOST MEMORABLE MOMENTS:

■ New Zealand's match against Italy as the 1987 tournament's opener wasn't a classic, but it did have an amazing moment. At the Italian restart, the kick-off was caught deep on the edge of the

All Blacks' 22 by Kiwi scrum-half David Kirk. Kirk then passed to Grant Fox deeper in their 22 for what should have been an automatic kick for touch. Instead Fox passed to winger John Kirwan on their own try-line. Not an ideal place to find yourself with the entire Italian side bearing down on you, you might think. It didn't seem to particularly bother the 6'3", 92-kg Kirwan though, as he decided to run the entire length of the field to score, handing off most of the Italian team on the way.

■ Minutes from the end of the 1987 Australia vs. France semi-final, the score stood at 24-24, the lead changing four times in the second half alone. With the clock ticking down, Sydney's Concord Oval crowd had resigned themselves to extra time. Then, despite receiving the ball deep in their 22, the French decided to run it out and started a move that saw the ball pass through eleven pairs of hands (props and all) before culminating in the injured Serge Blanco charging the last 30 metres down the touchline and diving full length into the corner ahead of four Australian backs. It was one of the greatest conclusions to one of the greatest games the World Cup has ever seen.

■ Having negotiated their way through the inaugural qualifying campaign for a place in the 1991 tournament, an unfancied Western Samoa made their debut against a Welsh team enjoying home advantage at Cardiff Arms Park and still riding high after their third-place finish in the previous World Cup. No amount of leek-throwing from the partisan crowd could stop the new-comers powering to a 16-13 victory. It was the first time a 'minnow' nation had beaten one of the eight founder members, and a great day for the future of the Rugby World Cup.

■ In 1991, Australia went to Lansdowne Road to face Ireland in the quarter-finals. In spite of Ireland's home advantage, everyone expected a relatively untroubled Australian progression to the last four. Everyone except the Irish, that is, and it turned out to be a genuine classic.

A huge punch-up between the two sets of forwards early in the first half set the tone in a match which saw two sides fight it out to the wire. Player of the Tournament David Campese scored twice, but twelve points from the boot of Irish fly-half Ralph Keyes ensured that the hosts remained in touch, but never ahead. Then, in the dying minutes, an Irish try by flanker Gordon Hamilton put the underdogs 18-15 ahead and saw Lansdowne Road erupt into mayhem.

Once the celebrating Dubliners had finally left the pitch, the game resumed, but with only moments remaining. The Wallabies kicked long at the restart, and continued pressure from their forwards eventually set up a scrum 15 metres out – and with it, one last chance. Michael Lynagh called his backs together to inform them of the play. They won the ball, which found its way into the hands of winger Campese. He cut infield, creating enough space for fly-half Lynagh to loop outside. Having wreaked sufficient havoc in the Irish defence, Campese passed out of the tackle to Lynagh, who scored in the far right-hand corner with absolutely no time left on the clock.

Lansdowne Road fell silent. The Wallabies had won by a point, had just avoided one of the greatest upsets in World Cup history, and were on their way to a semi-final with New Zealand and ultimately World Cup glory.

■ At Twickenham in 1991, England and Australia contested the second World Cup final. It was a peculiar afternoon in that England abandoned the style of tight forward play that had served them so well throughout the rest of the tournament. In spite of their pack clearly being on top in the match, England persisted with a running game that saw them trying to fling the ball wide to Jeremy Guscott and Rory Underwood at every possible opportunity.

Many fans thought this change of game-plan was in part due to goading – from the Australian camp in the week leading up to the final – of England's 'boring' style of play, notably by Australian winger David Campese, who spent the entire build-up rattling on about the 'beautiful game'.

For whatever reason they adapted their strategy, it didn't work, and late in the match they found themselves 12-3 down to an Australian side defending superbly. Then came a moment that possibly changed the destination of the William Webb Ellis Cup. With England very much in Australia's half, flanker Peter Winterbottom passed to Rory Underwood who, had he caught it, would have undoubtedly run in an England try. But the ball never reached Underwood, as the brilliant Campese reached out and deliberately knocked it on. Outraged as the Twickenham crowd was, they took refuge in the fact that the referee would surely award a penalty try and leave the home nation needing only one score to win or push the match to extra time. Derek Bevan took a long time to make his decision, but ended up awarding only a penalty.

Although Jon Webb successfully secured three points with his kick, it wasn't enough. It left England still needing a converted try, something they failed to achieve, leaving Australia to become World Champions for the first time.

■ At the start of the 1995 World Cup, hardly anyone had heard of a twenty-year-old New Zealand wing named Jonah Lomu. That was soon to change. Despite being 6'5" and 19 stone, he could run the 100m in 10.8 seconds. People had never seen anything like it, his preferred method being to run straight into or over any defender with the misfortune to get in his way.

It was England that was to feel the full fury of the bulldozing 'freak', as Will Carling labelled him. 'I have never prepared myself to be fifteen minutes into a game and know that it's basically over', complained Carling after the semi-final in which Lomu scored four phenomenal tries, including one in which he famously ran over a hapless Mike Catt. The next day, he reputedly started receiving seven-figure offers from a number of American football teams, none of which he accepted. Rugby's first global superstar was born.

■ Excluded from the first two World Cups as a result of the country's apartheid regime, South Africa's debut as hosts in 1995 provided one of the great moments of the late 20th century. Despite the final being won dramatically by the debutants late in extra time, the day will be remembered for a very different reason. Nelson Mandela, the new President of South Africa, a man who had suffered 26 years of political imprisonment at the hands of the apartheid regime before his release in 1990, emerged for the trophy presentation wearing a Springbok jersey, a once-potent symbol of that regime and the uniform for what had always been regarded as a white man's game. The 76-year-old waved to the crowd before giving the Cup to the white South African captain, François Pienaar, with the comment: 'François, I want to thank you for what you've done for this country.' His response was simple: 'Mr President, I want to thank you for what you've done.'

■ France vs. New Zealand, semi-final, 1999. Having picked up the Five Nations wooden spoon earlier the same year and been saved by some rather shoddy refereeing decisions against Fiji earlier in the tournament, you could say that France had been a tad fortunate to make it to the semi-final.

Having also taken a seven-try, 50-point drubbing from the All Blacks only four months before, it was less surprising then that the Kiwis took a convincing 24-10 lead. With Lomu on the rampage, having already scored two tries, it looked pretty much a done deal. Christophe Lamaison, the French fly-half, had other ideas, however, scoring 28 points in the match including a try, four conversions, three penalties and two drop goals as the French finished up eventual 43-31 winners. It was, and still is, the greatest comeback in World Cup rugby.

■ In 2003, South Africa comprehensively beat Samoa in the final match of the preliminary group stage. As Springbok fly-half Louis Koen kicked for goal towards the end of the game, a Samoan fan ran on to the pitch and tried to tackle him. Nevertheless, the fan knocked himself unconscious and Koen successfully converted his kick.

Eight pints of lager in an hour and being desperate for the toilet was the fan's later and relatively bizarre excuse.

■ In 2003, Australia and England met in the final at the Telstra Stadium in Sydney. With little more than a minute to go, and with the scores level at 17-17, England won a lineout just outside the Australian 22. Having been successfully caught by Lewis Moody at the back of the line-out, the ball found its way to scrum-half Matt Dawson, and then Mike Catt via Jonny Wilkinson. Catt surged forward but was enveloped by the Australian defence. A ruck formed, from which England successfully recycled the ball, allowing a characteristic dummy pass and dart forward by Dawson before he was tackled by the Australian centre Elton Flatley.

As various forwards piled in and another ruck formed, the drop goal was on. With Dawson buried in the middle of it all, flanker Neil Back found himself with the responsibility of sending the perfect pass to Wilkinson. Unsurprisingly perhaps, when you consider what was at stake, he chose a shorter pass into the hands of his captain Martin Johnson, who surged forward a few more yards. In the meantime, Dawson had emerged and resumed his role at scrum-half. With the ball waiting at the base of the ruck, and with Wilkinson in place, the moment had arrived.

In spite of a few Australians drifting offside, Dawson unleashed the pass to his fly-half. As the ball spun through the air towards Wilkinson, the English fans did their best to ignore the fact that he had already missed three drop goal attempts in the game. There wasn't going to be a fourth, however, and so – in the 99th minute and 33rd second of the match, and with his less favoured right foot – Wilkinson sent the ball sailing between the posts to give England a 20-17 victory and make him the tournament's highest scorer with 113 points.

Rugby Union's second global superstar had arrived, and England had won a world cup 37 years, 114 days, 17 hours and 53 minutes since their last, albeit in a different sport.

IT'S BEEN WON THE MOST TIMES BY:

Australia, who have won it twice and as a result affectionately refer to it as 'Bill'.

IT'S MADE OF:

Gilt silver.

HEIGHT:

38 cm.

BOOZE CAPACITY:

Not enough for most of the behemoths who usually end up drinking from it.

MANTELPIECE KUDOS:

On a par with telling women you're mates with Jonny Wilkinson.

CLEANING/MAINTENANCE REQUIRED:

Try to pronounce the names of the entire Welsh 1987 side 10–12 inches from cup, then wipe clean.

WHAT EVERY MAN WANTS

ESSENTIAL FACTS:

■ The highest international try-scorer of all time and goose-stepping serial Pommie-basher, David Campese, was forced to walk the length of London's Oxford Street wearing a sandwich board adorned with the words, 'I admit, the best team won', as a result of repeatedly writing off England's chances in 2003.

■ Naughty boys:

Most yellow cards in all World Cups: France – 5.
Most red cards in all World Cups: Canada – 3.

■ Had Jonny Wilkinson missed his drop goal at the end of the 2003 final, and neither team added to its score during the ten minutes of sudden-death, the destination of the Webb Ellis Cup would have been decided by five players from each side having a drop-kick competition. Wouldn't have been quite the same, would it?

■ Australia have scored only four drop goals in the history of the World Cup. Jonny Wilkinson scored eight by himself in 2003 alone.

■ The top ten all-time points-scoring nations in the Rugby World Cup:

1.	**New Zealand**	1,384
2.	**Australia**	987
3.	**France**	968
4.	**England**	957
5.	**Scotland**	770
6.	**Ireland**	610
7.	**South Africa**	556
8.	**Wales**	523
9.	**Argentina**	433
10.	**Samoa**	425

■ The inaugural World Cup in 1987 had a cumulative global television audience of 300 million viewers. By the following World Cup in 1991, that number had grown by 567 per cent to 1.75 billion. In 2003, it increased further still, doubling to 3.5 billion.

■ In the 1987 World Cup, the All Blacks scored a phenomenal 43 tries. They conceded four.

■ A list of all World Cup entrants – and for those that have them, their nicknames as well (spot the miserable teams from the UK who can't even muster a single nickname between them):

Argentina	Los Pumas
Australia	The Wallabies
Canada	The Canucks
England	
Fiji	
France	Les Bleus
Georgia	Lelos
Ireland	
Italy	Gli Azzurri
Ivory Coast	
Japan	The Cherry Blossoms
Namibia	
New Zealand	The All Blacks
Romania	The Oaks
Samoa	
Scotland	
Spain	Los Leones
South Africa	The Springboks
Tonga	'Ikale Tahi
Wales	
United States	The Eagles
Uruguay	Los Teros
Zimbabwe	

■ The same whistle has been blown to kick off every World Cup so far, but as it's almost 100 years old, the referee then has to revert to his own whistle, handing over the historic piece to an official at the first lineout.

The same coin is also used for the toss of the opening match. It's the coin used in the infamous England vs. New Zealand Test of 1925, in which, watched by 60,000 fans, the aforementioned whistle was blown in order to dismiss All Black forward Cyril Brownlie from the pitch, making him the first player ever to be sent off in an international match.

The story goes that the coin was lent for the toss in the 1925 game by All Black fan D.G. Gray, and so excited was he by its use that, after the match, he had a fern embossed on one side and a rose on the other. Apparently at the opening game of the 1991 World Cup, which saw the hosts England take on the defending champions New Zealand, both captains remained silent upon the toss, allowing the fern and the rose to decide.

■ Serge Blanco reputedly smoked 60 Gauloises a day throughout his career. That didn't stop him winning 93 international caps and scoring a French record 38 international tries.

■ Jonah Lomu has scored more Rugby World Cup tries than any other player. His total of fifteen was scored over two tournaments, eight of them in 1999, a record for one World Cup.

■ The top ten all-time points-scorers in the Rugby World Cup:

1. **Gavin Hastings** (SCO) 227
2. **Michael Lynagh** (AUS) 195
3. **Jonny Wilkinson** (ENG) 182
4. **Grant Fox** (NZL) 170
5. **Andrew Mehrtens** (NZL) 163
6. **Gonzalo Quesada** (ARG) 135
7. **Matt Burke** (AUS) 125
8. **Thierry Lacroix** (FRA) 124
9. **Gareth Rees** (CAN) 120
10. **Frédéric Michalak** (FRA) 103

THE CRICKET WORLD CUP

THE CRICKET WORLD CUP

AWARDED FOR WINNING:

The quadrennial world championship of cricket. Basically the biggest and best one-day cricket tournament on the planet.

CONTESTED BY:

The world's ten Test-playing nations plus six qualifiers.

A BRIEF HISTORY:

The cricketing world's first stab at an international competition came in the Triangular Tournament of 1912. It was a Test cricket competition played in England between the only Test-playing nations at the time – Australia, England and South Africa. Not helped by the inevitably useless British weather, interest from the public was lacklustre to say the least, ensuring that the tournament was never repeated.

The idea of a tournament of international cricket matches between more than two countries was not repeated until the advent of one-day International cricket and the inaugural Cricket World Cup in 1975. It was held in England and contested by the world's six Test-playing nations at the time – Australia, England, India, New Zealand, Pakistan and the West Indies – plus Sri Lanka and a composite team from East Africa. It was won by the West Indies, defeating Australia by seventeen runs in the final.

The following World Cup in 1979 was also held in England and saw the introduction of the ICC Trophy, the competition used to determine which non-Test-playing teams qualified for the main event. The World Cup itself was again won by the West Indies, when they defeated England by 92 runs in the final.

The third World Cup in 1983 was again held in England and was won by India, defeating the West Indies in the final by 43 runs.

1987 saw the tournament leave England for the first time. It was hosted by India and Pakistan, and it saw the West Indies fail to make the final for the first time. The final was contested by Australia and England, with Australia eventual winners by just seven runs, still the closest winning margin in a World Cup final so far.

The 1992 World Cup was co-hosted by Australia and New Zealand and ushered in a very new era in the tournament. It saw the introduction of white balls, coloured clothing and day–night matches. The fielding restrictions imposed during the first fifteen overs (stipulating that nine fielders had to be inside a 30-yard circle when the ball is bowled) also prompted the real deployment of the 'pinch hitter', notably New Zealand left-hander Mark Greatbatch, who was promoted up the batting order by his captain Martin Crowe because of his ability to score his runs predominantly in boundaries and so get their innings off to a flying start. Significantly, South Africa (having been readmitted to the International fold the previous year) also made their World Cup debut. The tournament was won by Pakistan, defeating England by 22 runs. In doing so, Pakistan had secured their first World Cup, and ensured that England had fallen at the final hurdle for the third time.

The 1996 World Cup was won amazingly by 66-1 outsiders Sri Lanka. They met tournament favourites Australia in the final and won comprehensively by seven wickets. The tournament had come to a successful conclusion, but not without its fair share of problems along the way. First, both Australia and the West Indies had refused to play their initial group games in Sri Lanka due to security fears in the wake of a terrorist bomb that had exploded in Colombo a fortnight before the start of the tournament, and as a result both forfeited their games. Although well on their way to victory anyway, Sri Lanka then had to be awarded a win in their semi-final against India by default, because of rioting in the 110,000-strong Calcutta crowd.

1999 saw the World Cup return to England after sixteen years, with some matches being played in Scotland, Ireland and Holland. Australia thrashed Pakistan in the final by eight wickets to claim their second Cricket World

Cup. That year also saw the introduction and awarding for the first time of the ICC Cricket World Cup Trophy, the first permanent prize in the history of the tournament.

It took a team of craftsmen at Garrard, the Crown Jewellers, more than 500 man-hours over a period of two months to create the gilded masterpiece. It features a golden globe shaped as a cricket ball, which is held up by three silver columns representing the three pillars of the game – batting, bowling and fielding. It has the names of the eight past winners inscribed on its base, and enough room for the next ten World Cups. What happens after that remains to be seen.

2003 saw the ICC Cricket World Cup Trophy contested for the second time, but not without a good dose of controversy. Shane Warne was sent home as the result of a positive drugs test before he'd even bowled a ball. A number of the Indian players threatened to pull out because of the embargo on personal sponsors. But the main issue under discussion was the political situation in Zimbabwe and whether teams should be playing in the country, given the alleged brutality of the Robert Mugabe regime. Two Zimbabwean players,

Andy Flower and Henry Olonga, came onto the pitch for their opening match wearing black armbands, having just released a statement explaining that they were 'mourning the death of democracy in our beloved Zimbabwe'.

In spite of all the problems, including the loss of the illustrious Warne, Australia romped through the tournament before thrashing India by 125 runs in the final and, in doing so, making themselves the nation to beat in the Caribbean in 2007 ...

MOST MEMORABLE MOMENTS:

■ In the 1979 final, Viv Richards walked out to the crease with the West Indies on 22. Several hours later he returned to the pavilion on 138 not out, having just dispatched the last ball into the Mound Stand for six to set England a target of 287 to win the World Cup.

In spite of Mike Brearley and Geoff Boycott getting off to a slow start, England seemed to be just about on target until they collapsed from 183 for 2 to 194 all out, with West Indian paceman Joel Garner taking five wickets in just eleven balls.

■ In 1983, Zimbabwe played in their first World Cup. It's difficult to see how a side could make more of an impact on their debut.

Zimbabwe had never even played an official one-day International before, let alone featured in the world's greatest cricket tournament. In contrast, their Australian opponents in their first match had no fewer than 476 one-day appearances between them. The scene was set for one of the biggest shocks in the history of the World Cup.

With a number of Zimbabwe wickets already down cheaply, and then Dave Houghton heading back to the pavilion with a golden duck, proceedings seemed to be going roughly as expected. Then Duncan Fletcher came to the crease. Although another wicket fell quickly at the other end, Fletcher steadied the ship before first putting on 70 with Kevin Curran and then 75 with Iain Butchart to help his side to a respectable 239.

Having done his bit with the bat, Fletcher then went to work with the ball. He dispatched the Australian openers in quick succession before later bagging another quick brace to leave the Aussies precariously placed at 133 for 4. Before long that was 138 for 5. Despite Australia losing only another couple of wickets, and despite Rod Marsh's quickfire unbeaten 50 from just 42 balls, the Zimbabwean bowlers restricted the favourites to 226 in their 60 overs, completing a result that only a few hours before no one would have possibly dreamed of.

The Zimbabwean team must have celebrated fairly hard that night, as they went on to lose their other five matches in the tournament. In fact, they had to wait until their last group match of the 1992 World Cup before securing their second one-day win.

■ In 1996, with only one professional cricketer in their ranks, Kenya took on the mighty West Indies, double winners of the World Cup. Somewhat unsurprisingly, then, the Kenyans were all out for 166, setting the West Indies little more than three runs an over to win.

Pretty much a done deal, you'd have thought. So did Maurice Odumbe, the Kenyan captain. 'We were going out for a picnic. It was only when they started to lose wickets that we began to get serious', he later said. Serious enough to eventually bowl the West Indies out for a paltry 93 and secure the biggest shock of the World Cup.

Man of the Match Odumbe later recalled: 'I met [Brian] Lara at a match in England several years ago before he was in the West Indies team and asked for his autograph. He said he didn't have time. When we beat them in the World Cup I went up to him and said, "A few years ago I asked for your autograph and you wouldn't give it. Now I am saying you can have mine."'

Eat that, Brian.

■ At one point during the 1996 India vs. Pakistan quarter-final, Pakistani batsman Aamer Sohail hit Venkatesh Prasad through a vacant part of the field for four runs. Sohail pointed at Prasad, and then to the gap in the field to indicate that, in the absence of a nearby fielder, the bowler should retrieve the ball himself. The very next delivery, Prasad bowled Sohail, and then wasted no time in pointing him to the pavilion.

■ In 1999 Australia met India at The Oval in a Super Six match. It soon became apparent that, other than trying to progress to the semi-finals, both sides were doing their best to rid London of its pigeons as well.

An extraordinary ten minutes got under way when the ball was hit down to Aussie medium pacer Paul Reiffel at the third-man boundary. Reiffel picked up the ball and threw it back into the stumps – only for it to knock a passing bird from the sky, allowing the Indian batsmen to grab another run.

Then, while on 99, India's Ajay Jadeja cut a ball that looked set to evade all the Aussie fielders and bring up his century, except another pigeon had chosen to stand in its way. Although it brilliantly saved the single and denied Jadeja his century, the bird gave its life in the process.

Among all the feathery carnage, Jadeja eventually made it to a century, but that didn't stop the Australians winning by 77 runs.

■ Whether apocryphal or not, probably the most famous comment ever made on a cricket pitch came from the Australian captain Steve

Waugh in an epic Super Six clash between Australia and South Africa at the World Cup in 1999.

South Africa looked to be well on their way to victory in the game when, to make matters worse for the Australians, Steve Waugh popped a sitter straight to Herschelle Gibbs at midwicket. In his excitement at the prospect of inflicting what would probably have been the killer blow to Australian prospects, Gibbs tried to celebrate the catch too early, and as he went to throw the ball in the air, it spilled from his hand and onto the ground.

Legend has it that as Waugh passed Gibbs he asked the distraught South African: 'How does it feel to have dropped the World Cup?' Whether it's true or not, we do know that Waugh then went on to an unbeaten and match-winning 120 with just two balls to spare, and then captained his country to World Cup glory a few days later.

■ Canada are very much a minnow of World Cup cricket. They have played in two World Cups so far, posting the record lowest scores in both. Bearing this in mind will help you realise the significance of Canada's John Davison leathering a

67-ball century against the West Indies in 2003. It was the fastest century in World Cup history, included six sixes, and came to an end only from Vasbert Drakes' catch – one of the best ever seen on a cricket field. Davison, in order to underline that his innings wasn't a fluke, then proceeded to smash a half-century against New Zealand, including a six so big that it landed on the neighbouring golf course.

■ When Sri Lanka played Bangladesh in 2003, Chaminda Vaas made World Cup history by taking three wickets with the very first three balls of the game. As if that wasn't enough, he got his fourth by the end of the over, leaving Bangladesh on 5 for 4 and well on their way to a ten-wicket defeat. Vaas went on to be the tournament's leading wicket-taker.

■ In 2003, Kenya became the first non-Test-playing nation to get beyond the group stage of the World Cup. In fact, they beat 1996 World Champions Sri Lanka and got to the semi-finals. On their return, they could barely get out of Jomo Kenyatta International Airport for the thousands of adoring fans who came to give them a welcome fitting of their achievement.

■ When the West Indies played Sri Lanka in 2003, Ramnaresh Sarwan scored 47. Now that may not seem like a particularly big score, but in order to complete his innings, Sarwan had to discharge himself from hospital. Early in his innings, he was hit on the head by a bouncer and rushed to A & E. In spite of medical advice to the contrary, Sarwan hastily returned to the ground and steered his side to within a whisker of an unlikely victory.

■ There aren't many cricketing stages bigger than a World Cup semi-final, but that didn't stop Australian Adam Gilchrist from walking during the match with Sri Lanka in 2003. The umpire didn't hear the nick, but Gilchrist headed for the pavilion nonetheless.

■ When the Australians emphatically won the 2003 World Cup, they became only the second side to go through the entire competition undefeated. This achievement was particularly impressive in that 2003 was the longest tournament so far, with Australia having to play eleven matches before becoming eventual winners. They did, however, save the best until last.

In the final in Johannesburg, Australia batted first, setting India 359 – the fourth-highest total in World Cup history and the highest ever in a final. Ricky Ponting made an unbeaten 140 (the highest in a World Cup final) which included eight sixes (a record in any match in any World Cup). With Damien Martyn, who was also unbeaten on 88, he put together a partnership of 234 (a World Cup final record). Their stand was also only four runs short of the all-time World Cup record for a third-wicket partnership, but as they made it in just 30 overs, and Martyn had a broken finger, we can probably let them off.

IT'S BEEN WON THE MOST TIMES BY:

Australia have won it three times, the West Indies have won it twice, and India, Pakistan and Sri Lanka have all won it once.

IT'S MADE OF:

Gilt silver and wood.

HEIGHT:

60.2 cm.

WEIGHT:

11,102 g.

PRIZE MONEY THAT COMES WITH IT:

When Australia won the trophy in 2003, they also took a rather handy US$2 million home with them as well.

MANTELPIECE KUDOS:

Unlikely to impress your grandfather who no doubt still regards one-day cricket as evil, corrupting filth (but probably spends the entire Lord's Test asleep dribbling down his MCC tie).

ESSENTIAL FACTS:

■ The highest team total in the World Cup: 398 for 5 (50.0 overs) – Sri Lanka vs. Kenya in 1996.

■ The lowest team total in the World Cup: 36 (18.4 overs) – Canada vs. Sri Lanka in 2003.

■ After Australia beat New Zealand in the 1987 World Cup, the Aussies got up at 6 am the following day to train on the front lawn of their hotel – so the Kiwis would see them as they boarded the coach to the airport.

■ The strike rate (the average number of runs per 100 balls faced) for South African Lance Klusener from his eleven World Cup innings is 121.17 – better than any other batsman to have graced the tournament in its history. He also has the highest batting average in any World Cup, with 140.5 in 1999.

■ In 1996, South Africa's Gary

Kirsten hammered an unbeaten 188 runs from a hapless bowling attack from the United Arab Emirates. It remains the Cricket World Cup's highest individual score.

■ India's Sachin Tendulkar has scored 1,732 runs in the World Cup – more than any other player.

■ In the 1987 World Cup, Australia played India in their opening game. Australia batted first and at one point during their innings, Aussie No. 3 Dean Jones hit Maninder Singh for what the batsman thought was a six.

Umpire Dickie Bird was unsure and so asked Ravi Shastri, who was fielding on the boundary, who said it was only a four. Dickie Bird took his word for it and so awarded a four.

The Aussies complained about the decision after their innings, having seen the replay on television. In response, Dickie Bird asked Ravi Shastri again, who this time admitted that it might have cleared the boundary rope for a six.

The Australian total was adjusted from 269 to 271, which turned out to be fairly important, as the team ended up winning the match by one run.

■ In 1996, Australia's Mark Waugh became the only batsman to hit three centuries in a World Cup.

■ The fastest delivery ever recorded was bowled in a preliminary group match between Pakistan and England in the 2003 World Cup. Pakistan's Shoaib Akhtar fired the ball down at the unfortunate Nick Knight at 100.2 mph (161.3 km/h)!

■ Pakistan's Wasim Akram has taken 55 wickets in the World Cup – more than any other player.

■ In the first-ever World Cup cricket match on 7 June 1975, the great Indian opening batsman Sunil Gavaskar batted through his country's entire 60-over innings for just 36 runs. It would probably be fair to say that the Indian side hadn't really got the idea behind one-day cricket at that point. Chasing England's 334, they managed just 132 but still had seven wickets in hand at the end of their innings.

■ In 1983, India's Kapil Dev hit an unbeaten 175 against Zimbabwe in what was one of the all-time great World Cup innings. However, it was lost to posterity as the BBC had gone on strike that day, and so there's no footage of it whatsoever.

■ In 1996, Javed Miandad became the first and only player to have taken part in all six World Cups up to that point.

■ India have a 100 per cent record against Pakistan in the Cricket World Cup.

■ At 21 years and 75 days, Australia's Ricky Ponting was the youngest player to score a World Cup century – an unbeaten record. He has also taken more catches as a fielder than any other player, with eighteen.

■ England have used more players in the World Cup than any other nation.

■ Best bowling figures in a World Cup match: 7 for 15 – Australia's Glenn McGrath vs. Namibia in 2003.

■ Best bowling economy rate in the World Cup (qualification 500 balls): 2.66 — England's Bob Willis.

■ Best bowling strike rate in the World Cup (minimum qualification fifteen wickets): 19.43 — the West Indies' V.C. Drakes.

■ Namibian bowling all-rounder Rudi van Vuuren played in the 2003 Cricket World Cup. Nothing particularly amazing about that, you might think, except that he also represented his country in the Rugby World Cup later that year.

■ Pakistan played so badly in the 2003 World Cup that the players were fined half their tournament earnings.

BEST KEPT:

Wherever you want — it's been deliberately designed with platonic dimensions whereby it looks pretty much the same (or is certainly instantly recognisable) from whichever angle it's viewed.

THE YELLOW JERSEY

THE YELLOW JERSEY

AWARDED FOR LEADING AND ULTIMATELY WINNING:

Le Tour de France – a ridiculously epic three-week bicycle stage race contested over more than 2,000 miles of road in and around France – unquestionably the world's single most physiologically demanding sporting event.

CONTESTED BY:

200 professional yet reasonably mad cyclists, making it the world's largest annual pro-sporting event.

A BRIEF HISTORY:

The Tour was founded as a marketing stunt to save the newspaper *L'Auto* (ancestor of the present *L'Equipe*) by its editor and co-founder,

Henri Desgrange. It had been inspired by a novel, *Tour de France par Deux Enfants*, in which two boys make their way around France, and was first suggested as an idea by journalist Géo Lefèvre to his editor Desgrange over lunch at the Café de Madrid in Paris on 20 November 1902.

On 19 January 1903, *L'Auto* announced 'the greatest cycling trial in the entire world. A race more than a month long: Paris to Lyon to Marseille to Toulouse to Bordeaux to Nantes to Paris.' With a 20-franc entry fee, response was poor. Only fifteen riders had entered by a week before the scheduled 31 May start, forcing Desgrange to postpone the race to 1 July, increase the prize money to 20,000 francs, and announce that the first 50 riders were to be given 5 francs a day for expense money. That seemed to do the trick, and within a short time 60 cyclists had signed up. Even though logistical issues forced a further delay to 19 July, the race turned out to be a considerable success. It saw the 60 riders travelling 2,500 km (1,550 miles) over nineteen days on the basic cycle machinery of the time, a lot of it through the night. Its gruelling schedule added to the event's draw, and by the time the winner Maurice Garin entered Paris, he was greeted by a crowd of 20,000 paying spectators. Daily circulation of *L'Auto* leapt from 25,000 before the 1903 Tour to 65,000 after it.

The successful format of a race through the country, broken into stages and based on cumulative time, has remained intact to this day. However, Desgrange felt that interest could be sustained only if the course changed each year, so in 1910 he spiced things up a bit by adding a stage through the Pyrenees. As if that wasn't enough, the following year he sent the poor buggers through the Alps as well. The itinerary of the race continues to change each year, clockwise around France one year and anti-clockwise the next.

As successful a spectacle as the Tour was right from the very start, Desgrange was concerned that the enjoyment for the hordes of people who lined each stage to watch the riders pass was hindered by the fact that they very often didn't know who was winning. During the 1919 Tour, while pondering the problem on the rest day in Luchon, it occurred to Desgrange that all that was needed was a solitary piece of distinguishable clothing. On 10 July 1919, he announced that it was to be a yellow jersey, the colour having been decided by the yellow paper that *L'Auto* was printed on. Although pretty much inspired by the prospect of selling some newspapers, no one can deny that it has become won of the most prized possessions in sport.

MOST MEMORABLE MOMENTS:

■ In 1913, while descending the Tourmalet and wearing the yellow jersey, Eugène Christophe crashed heavily, breaking the front fork on his bicycle. Having already covered 200 km (125 miles) up and down mountains that day – and now nursing a serious injury as a result of his crash – he was left with no option but to carry his bike and run ten miles to the nearest village, where he single-handedly repaired his bike in the local blacksmith's before setting off again to eventually finish the stage deep into the night.

As if he wasn't having a bad enough day already, the race officials deemed a slight pumping of the bellows for him by the blacksmith's apprentice as outside help, and he was handed a further three-minute time penalty.

■ In 1929, yellow jersey-wearer Victor Fontan suffered a similar stage from hell when he crashed in the Pyrenees, also breaking the front fork of his bike. To make matters worse, there was a rule that year stipulating that a rider had to finish a stage with the same bike he started with. With his own bike beyond repair, Fontan knocked on the doors of nearby houses to see if anyone would lend him theirs. He eventually found one, and in a rather nice interpretation of the rules, rode the remaining 90 miles of the stage with his broken bike strapped to his back.

■ In 1935, Spanish racer Francesco Cepeda died after plunging down a ravine on the descent of the Col du Galibier in the French Alps. The Tour had suffered its first racing victim.

■ In 1967, while challenging for the yellow jersey, England's Tom Simpson broke away from the pack early on the ascent of Mont Ventoux. It was a fiercely hot day, and it's thought that Simpson had drunk brandy earlier in the stage to combat the effects of a stomach bug that he was carrying. To compound the issue, he was racing in the days when the amount of water allowed was limited, often forcing riders to stop and fill their bottles at fountains or sneakily raid a roadside bar or café.

Around a mile short of the summit, Simpson began to waver, meandering back and forth across the road, before falling over on his bike. In spite of his team car helpers' efforts to get him to retire from the race at this point, Simpson insisted that they help him back onto his bike so he could carry on. A couple of hundred metres later, though, he began to slowly drift to the right of the road, before again falling from his bike and into the hands of his following helpers. Simpson had died from heart failure chasing the yellow jersey, and England had lost probably the greatest road bicycle racer it has ever produced.

Reluctant to continue so soon after the death of a fellow competitor, the following day the riders asked for a delay before resuming the race. Tour organisers declined the idea, but the field agreed to race only on the condition that they would allow an Englishman to win the stage in honour of the late Simpson.

Amphetamines and alcohol were later found in Simpson's bloodstream, ushering in a new era which has seen widespread drug-testing within the sport.

■ In 1971, while in battle with the legendary Eddy Merckx, Luis Ocaña was left lying on the roadside in his torn yellow jersey after sliding out on a switchback near the foot of the Col de Menté during a violent electrical storm in the Pyrenees. Merckx, in a noble gesture, declined to don the jersey the morning after Ocaña was forced to pull out of the Tour.

■ In the final stage of the 1989 Tour, Paris watched in horror as American Greg LeMond set the fastest stage time in Tour history and overcame a 50-second deficit to beat Frenchman Laurent Fignon's overall lead by just eight seconds. Don't forget that's an eight-second difference after three weeks of racing over more than 2,000 miles. Unsurprisingly, it's still the closest winning margin in the Tour's history.

■ On 18 July 1995, Italian rider Fabio Casartelli and a number of other competitors crashed at 60 mph on the descent of the Col de Portet d'Aspet in the Pyrenees. Casartelli's head struck a large concrete block at the side of the road designed to stop cars from falling down the mountain, and he tragically died while being taken to hospital by helicopter.

After much deliberation, his team decided to continue in the Tour. On the next stage, they were left to cross the finish line in first place, side by side, in honour of their dead team-mate, with the peloton following slowly behind. Two days later, on stage eighteen, Lance Armstrong found himself in a small breakaway group up front before going on to win the stage. As he approached the line, he pointed up to the sky as a way of dedicating the win to his dead friend.

On 22 October of the same year, Casartelli's new son Fabio was baptised in the chapel at Madonna del Ghisallo, a hill close to Lake Como in Italy. Casartelli's crumpled bike is placed in the shrine at the chapel in his memory.

In 1997 the Col de Portet d'Aspet was incorporated into the Tour's route again, and riders stopped for a brief moment where he had crashed to honour the Italian, before continuing with the stage.

■ In October 1996, American Lance Armstrong was diagnosed with testicular cancer so advanced that it had already spread to his lungs and brain. Doctors told him that he had a less than 40 per cent chance of living, but later admitted (once he had recovered) that it was in fact far lower, and that he had been given the inflated figure as a means of giving him hope.

Following the amputation of a testicle and the removal of the brain tumours, Armstrong underwent a ferocious programme of chemotherapy. The standard course of chemotherapy for his level of stage three cancer would have spelled the end of his cycling career, as it came with a profound reduction in lung capacity as a known side-effect. So, instead, Armstrong opted for a stronger and more dangerous treatment, the upside being that it was less likely to damage his lungs.

The gamble paid off, and as the cancer began to subside, Armstrong resumed training. But he no longer had a team contract that would enable him to compete. Eventually, in 1998, the newly-formed United States Postal Service Pro Cycling Team signed him – which turned out to be a rather astute move on their part, as he won the Tour de France the following year. 'The obligation of the cured', as he called it, drove him to seven consecutive Tour victories before retiring in 2005, finally allowing someone else to win what had come to be known as the 'Tour de Lance'.

IT'S BEEN WON THE MOST TIMES BY:

The Tour has been won the most times by Lance Armstrong (USA) – 7. But to complicate matters, the most career yellow jerseys for leading stages of the Tour and winning it as well is held by Belgium's Eddy Merckx with 111, whereas Armstrong is second with 83.

IT'S MADE OF:

Synthetic stuff – some of the same material they make space shuttle tiles out of, apparently.

WEIGHT:

Space shuttles seem to stay up in the air most of the time, so I guess it's fairly light.

BOOZE CAPACITY:

None, but that's no bad thing, as Tom Simpson definitively illustrated. Having said that, the leader, if far enough ahead going into the last stage through the streets of Paris, usually nails a glass or two of bubbly along the way.

PRIZE MONEY THAT COMES WITH IT:

450,000 euros.

COATHANGER KUDOS:

Pretty damn hip. Avoid ties.

CLEANING/MAINTENANCE REQUIRED:

A sympathetic detergent.

ESSENTIAL FACTS:

■ Riders who successfully complete the Tour cover in the region of 2,300 miles at an average speed of 25 mph (40 km/h). That's roughly the equivalent of running a marathon pretty much every day for three weeks.

■ Released on their 1978 album *Jazz*, Queen's hit song 'Bicycle Race' was inspired by the Tour de France. Freddie Mercury decided to write it having watched the Tour pass the French hotel he was staying in.

For the single's video, the band staged a bicycle race contested by 65 naked girls around a race track. The video was initially banned until re-edited. The bikes used had been hired from Harrods, and reputedly the world-famous store was insistent that the band buy the seats, once they learned what they had been used for.

The single was released as a double A-side with the song 'Fat Bottomed Girls'.

■ In the mountain stages in the Alps and Pyrenees, riders climb a vertical distance the equivalent of three Mount Everests stacked on top of each other.

■ Legend has it that any rider who has worn the yellow jersey, even for a day, will never go hungry or thirsty in France again.

■ Riders consume about 10,000 calories per day – or, put another way, the same as eating just under eighteen Big Macs. This calorific intake, coupled with the level of activity and energy expended, increases the average rider's metabolic rate to a level exceeded by only four species on earth.

■ There is a vehicle that follows all the riders on each stage, picking up anyone who has fallen too far behind. It was introduced to the Tour after mountain stages were added in 1910, and is called the *voiture balai* or broom wagon, based on the fact that its job is to 'sweep up' any riders littering the track. In the past, the vehicle had broom bristles attached to the front bumper, or sometimes a whole broom attached to its side.

■ Other coloured jerseys awarded to riders and what they represent:

• **Green jersey** – goes to the most consistent finisher. Points are awarded each day for position, rather than time, across the finish line. The green jersey is worn in the Tour by the highest points scorer, and is generally won by a sprint specialist. It was first awarded in 1953 to celebrate the Tour's 50th anniversary.

• **Polka dot jersey** – points are awarded on the mountain stages of the Tour, based on position and difficulty of climb, and the polka dot jersey is worn by the rider with the most accumulated points picked up in the mountains. It is also

known as the King of the Mountains jersey, and was introduced in 1975.

• **Red jersey** – no longer used, but previously awarded to the rider with most points picked up in intermediate sprints during stages. Last used in 1989.

• **Combination jersey** – a patchwork design of the yellow, green, red and polka dot jerseys, awarded to the leader of a points system based on the categories for all of them. Also abolished in 1989.

• **White jersey** – the equivalent of the yellow jersey, but available only to riders under 25 years old on 1 January in the year the Tour is contested. Since 1996 it has been known as the Souvenir Fabio Casartelli, in honour of the rider who died on the descent of the Col de Portet d'Aspet the year before.

• **Rainbow jersey** – worn by the reigning world champion, the winner of the one-day road race World Cycling Championship held each year in early October. The holder is entitled to wear the jersey for a year, although if he becomes leader in the Tour, the yellow jersey takes precedence.

■ In 1969 Eddy Merckx won not only the yellow jersey, but the green and polka dot jerseys as well. This is the only time in the history of the Tour that this has been achieved. Had the white jersey been available at the time, he would have won that as well.

■ Competitors in the Tour follow an elaborate but unwritten code of honour – whenever reasonably possible, a rider will be left to lead the prevailing pack on his birthday or when the race passes through his home village. It is also no coincidence that the winner of the stage held on Bastille Day is very often French.

■ As overall victory in the Tour is based on accumulative time, it means you can win the whole thing without winning a single individual stage. Although it's highly unlikely, as there are around twenty stages, this was achieved by American Greg LeMond in 1990.

■ The last placed rider is known as the *lanterne rouge* in reference to the red light found on the back of trains. To come in last often requires more skill than you would have thought – the position carries more prestige and attracts far more publicity than the rider who comes second from last. As a result, down the years, many riders have deliberately engineered themselves into last place in the closing stages in a number of elaborate and bizarre ways.

■ Three competitors were disqualified in the fourth Tour de France in 1906 when caught taking a train as a shortcut.

■ A stage in Plymouth in 1974 saw the Tour's first visit to England.

■ Riders today don't know they're born. When the Tour started in 1903, there were only six stages, as opposed to the twenty that comprise the event today. As a result, the stages were a lot longer. They averaged over 400 km (250 miles), ensuring that several were completed deep into the night. Some stages were even started during the night to cater for the ridiculous duration; the longest of these took 27 hours and 47 minutes for a rider to win.

■ In the Tour's early years, the event was plagued by amused spectators who put nails in the road into the path of oncoming cyclists.

■ At a border-hugging 5,745 km (3,560 miles), the 1926 Tour was the longest in the history of the race. Not content with making the competitors go through the Alps once at the beginning of the Tour, the organisers made them climb them again at the end as well.

■ In 1928, in his second consecutive win of the Tour, Nicolas Frantz became only the second rider to wear the yellow jersey for the entire race. Rather impressive in itself, but especially so when you consider that at one point the

frame of his bicycle broke, leaving him no option but to borrow an undersized women's bike to get him the 100 km to the end of the stage.

■ In 1914, the twelfth Tour began on the same day that Franz Ferdinand, Archduke of Austria, was assassinated in Sarajevo, marking the start of the First World War. Four previous winners of the Tour were to die on the battlefields of Europe.

ONE SIZE FITS ALL?

■ In one year, the tallest rider competing for the yellow jersey was 6'5.5", with the shortest being 5'2".

■ In one year, the heaviest rider competing for the yellow jersey was 14st 14lb, with the lightest 8st 14lb.

BEST KEPT:

Away from fire.

THE RYDER CUP

THE RYDER CUP

AWARDED FOR WINNING:

A biennial golfing event officially called the Ryder Cup Matches. Basically the biggest and best team golf event in the world.

CONTESTED BY:

Originally by teams from America and Great Britain, but after 45 years of US dominance (Britain won only once between 1935 and 1973), it was extended to Britain and Ireland in 1973, and then all of continental Europe in 1979.

A BRIEF HISTORY:

No one can still quite decide who came up with the concept to stage international matches between the best professionals in America and those of Great Britain, but regardless of who should take the credit, the first informal matches were played at Gleneagles, Scotland in 1921. They were played just before the 2,000 Guineas Match

Play Championship, with the British soundly beating the US team 9-3.

In 1926, the Royal and Ancient Golf Club (R&A) imposed qualifying rounds for the Open Championship, which forced any American entrants to make their transatlantic trek for the tournament a little earlier. With some time to kill, the Americans formed a team and took on a British team at Wentworth in another unofficial match which the Americans again lost, this time in a 13½ to 1½ drubbing.

Watching the match unfold was one Samuel A. Ryder, an Englishman from St Albans in Hertfordshire. Ryder was a very wealthy man, having started his own very successful business selling penny seed packets. When he had become ill from overwork while making his fortune, the doctors had prescribed fresh air and light exercise and had actively encouraged him to take up golf. Devoted to cricket, he initially spurned the idea, but in time relented. He employed the services of the British star Abe Mitchell as his personal coach, and before long was hooked, practising religiously six days a week (but never on a Sunday).

He relished watching the match at Wentworth in 1926, and afterwards had a drink with some of the competitors, including Mitchell and American star Walter Hagen. During the evening it was suggested that the fixture should be established on a more regular and official basis. Ryder took to the idea with gusto. He immediately pledged to donate a cup, and to 'give £5 to each of the winning players, and give a party afterwards, with champagne and chicken sandwiches!'

True to his word, Ryder commissioned Mappin & Webb to make a solid gold trophy to the value of £250. He insisted that a figure of a golfer adorn the lid and that it resemble his friend and coach Abe Mitchell. The first official Ryder Cup was then arranged to take place at the Worcester Country Club, Massachusetts on 3 and 4 June 1927. Although the appeal to raise £3,000 to fund the players was met with apathy and fell £500 short, Ryder happily made up the deficit, and the British team were on their way. The inaugural Ryder Cup was comprehensively won by the US 9½ to 2½, and the fixture continued to be played biennially until its suspension during

1939–45 for the Second World War. Samuel Ryder lived to see his trophy presented twice on his home soil before sadly dying on 2 January 1936. He was 77. There is no other man who – having taken an interest in golf at such a late stage in his life – has produced such a fantastic legacy for the game.

When the Ryder Cup matches resumed after the war, it became very apparent in the following decades that the limited pool of British players were on the whole no match for the hugely dominant Americans. With the exception of the famous tie at Royal Birkdale in 1969, the US had won every event from 1959 until 1973, and so it was decided that the British team would be expanded to include Ireland. Despite the change, America still continued to dominate, and so in 1979, with the blessing of the Ryder family, the selection procedure was changed again to include all of Europe. Although the US still won the following three events, the Ryder Cup had become the more competitive and compelling contest we enjoy today.

In 2001, eight days after the

September 11 attacks across America, it was decided that the Ryder Cup would be re-scheduled to the following year, with all future matches contested in even-numbered years.

MOST MEMORABLE MOMENTS:

■ In 1931, in his match against Great Britain's Fred Robson at the Scioto Country Club, Ohio, American Gene Sarazen hit one of his tee shots over the green and into a drinks hut behind. Robson, whose ball had landed on the green 25 feet from the pin, waited patiently as Sarazen entered the hut, where he found that his ball had come to a rest in a large crack on the cement floor beside a rather large fridge. As the American leant down to pick it up and concede the hole, he noticed a little open window that faced the green. Ridiculously difficult as the shot was, the match was close, and so Sarazen sought some assistance to move the fridge before giving it a go. And so, with an awkward stance, a nearby fridge and a restricted backswing, Sarazen chipped the ball through the window and on to the green, only ten feet from the hole. Rattled by the American's recovery, Robson three-putted and Sarazen went on to win the match 7 and 6.

■ In 1957, on the final day at Lindrick Golf Club in Yorkshire, British captain Dai Rees decided to drop Harry Weetman and Max Faulkner from the singles. Weetman was furious and sulked, whereas Faulkner still felt he had a part to play. Before the days of leader boards or other means of communication on the course, Faulkner took it upon himself to run from match to match to report the progress of his team. Inspired by Faulkner's efforts, the British won six out of eight of their singles matches and secured the Ryder Cup. Many of the British team credited Faulkner for their victory.

■ At the height of American domination of the event, 1969 saw the most closely contested and perhaps the best Ryder Cup to date, with eighteen of the 32 matches going to the last green. In spite of this, it will undoubtedly be remembered for the most phenomenal moment of sportsmanship that the competition

– and perhaps golf played at the highest level – has ever seen.

Although playing in his first Ryder Cup, Jack Nicklaus was selected for the pivotal final singles match on the final day. Despite carrying the hopes of the entire US nation on his shoulders, he was still all-square with Open Championship-holder Tony Jacklin when they arrived at the 18th green. Nicklaus then set up a possible win by sinking a nerve-shredding four-foot putt for par. It meant that Jacklin had to sink his difficult three-footer to secure a half on the hole, halve the game and tie the whole match. Instead, as Nicklaus picked his ball from the hole he also picked up Jacklin's marker, conceding the putt and creating the first tie in the history of the Ryder Cup. 'I don't think you would have missed it', said Nicklaus quietly to Jacklin, 'but in these circum-stances I would never give you the opportunity.'

It became apparent that Nicklaus's captain Sam Snead and several of his team-mates were less than impressed. 'I believed good sportsman-ship should be as much a part of the Ryder Cup as great competition' was Nicklaus's characteristi-cally impressive response.

■ In 1975 at the Laurel Valley Golf Club, Pennsylvania, the US team charged to a comprehensive 21-11 victory which included an 11-5 singles margin on the final day. It could have been greater but for the biggest upset in Ryder Cup history. Jack Nicklaus had arrived at the 1975 Ryder Cup having just won his fifth Masters in April, his fourth PGA Championship in August and the World Open at Pinehurst. By his own admission, he was playing 'the best golf of his life'. But he was beaten in the singles not once but twice, and both times by the same man.

'I know how bloody mad he was, but he never showed it and congratulated me warmly', said Englishman Brian Barnes after his morning 4 and 2 victory over Nicklaus. 'We talked fishing a lot of the way round, and you know, Jack was responsible for rematching us again in the afternoon. America had won the Cup by then and it was he who suggested to Arnold Palmer, their captain, that the order of play should be fiddled so that we met again. It gave the crowd something to watch and I remember Jack saying to me on the first tee:

"You've beaten me once, but there ain't no way you're going to beat me again." And then he started – birdie, birdie, and I didn't think I would. But I did.'

Barnes kept in touch with the mercurial Nicklaus before edging into the lead with birdies on the 11th and 12th. In spite of pressure from the American throughout the back nine, Barnes, with pipe firmly in mouth, held on to win 2 and 1.

Years later, Barnes revealed that from that moment on, he couldn't go anywhere without someone asking him what it felt like to beat the great Jack Nicklaus twice in a day.

■ In 1983, at the PGA National, Florida, Seve Ballesteros and Fuzzy Zoeller came to the 18th tee all square. Both players then hit their drives into the deep rough. While Zoeller successfully managed a recovery shot out onto the fairway, the hapless Ballesteros could only hack his ball 25 yards into a nearby bunker. With the game looking lost, Ballesteros pulled out his 3-wood, and from the sand hit a cut shot with a huge amount of deliberate slice to within fifteen feet of the flag. No one could quite believe it. Jack Nicklaus, captain of the American team that year, simply described it as 'the finest shot I have ever seen', and Ballesteros went on to secure an unlikely yet vital half point.

■ Having accused each other of cheating at the Belfry in 1989, it appeared that American Paul Azinger and Spaniard Seve Ballesteros were not about to let sleeping dogs lie when they went to Kiawah Island two years later. 'I can tell you, we're not trying to cheat', Azinger claimed. 'Oh no. Breaking the rules and cheating are two different things', was the European's response.

The brazenly open needle between the two players, and the resultant desire to win with their partners (Chip Beck and José María Olazábal) at any cost, led to what is widely regarded as the best pairs match in history, the Spaniards eventually winning 2 and 1.

■ Kiawah Island in 1991 also saw the most serious collapse in an individual's game in the history of the Ryder Cup. Four up with four to play, and cruising against a hapless Colin Montgomerie, Mark Calcavecchia's game began to fall apart. He lost the 15th, then the 16th, then hit his tee shot into the water to lose the par-3 17th, before finally losing the 18th and allowing Montgomerie to secure a vitally important half point that led to one of the most nerve-shredding climaxes ever seen in sport.

The Ryder Cup matches that year went to the final shot on the final green of the final match on the final day. American Hale Irwin, upon realising the significance of his final singles match with German Bernhard Langer, later said: 'I couldn't breathe, I couldn't swallow, I couldn't do any-thing.' As a result, on the 18th, he pushed his approach shot to the green very right and clattered into a hole-side spectator. He followed it up with a poor chip shot, but then superbly putted to within a foot of the hole. The unfalter-ingly nerveless and reliable Langer conceded Irwin's putt. Forty-five feet from the pin, Langer had two putts to get down, win the match, draw the overall team scores level, and retain the Ryder Cup for Europe. He hit his first six feet past. Slightly peculiarly, many people in the greenside galleries decided not to watch. They couldn't. Langer and his caddie understandably took some time lining up the shot before the German finally stepped up to the ball. It felt like about ten minutes. The second putt shaved the right hand side of the cup but went past.

'I saw two spike marks on my line', said Langer later. 'It looked like a left-left putt. I talked to my caddie. He said, "Hit it left-centre and firm to avoid the spike marks. That's what I tried to do. It did not go in.'

He was right. It hadn't gone in, and the Americans had won the 'War on the Shore' – and with it, had got back the Ryder Cup.

■ The final day at the Belfry in 1993 saw virtual stalemate in the singles games and in the overall score right across the board. Then, in the final game, all square and with five holes left to play, Nick Faldo hit a 6-iron off the tee which landed on the green, rolled up the hill and dropped into the hole. You could say that it was rather good timing to shoot only the second hole-in-one that the Ryder Cup matches had ever seen.

■ The 1999 Ryder Cup at The

Country Club in Brookline, Massachusetts saw a remarkable conclusion for very different reasons. The American team went into the singles on the final day trailing 10-6. No one can deny that their comeback – by going 8-3-1 in the singles matches to bring about a 14½ to 13½ victory – was impressive. In fact, it was the greatest comeback on the final day in Ryder Cup history. It was a shame, therefore, that their celebrations didn't strike a similarly impressive note.

It came down to the 17th hole of a match between American Justin Leonard and Spaniard José María Olazábal. Leonard, 1-up going down the par-4 17th, needed to win one of the last two holes or halve both to secure an American victory. Olazábal hit his second to leave himself with a 22-foot birdie putt. Leonard then hit his second to within ten feet of the hole, but had to watch in horror as it rolled back down the green before finally coming to a stop 45 feet from the flag in the shadow of an overhanging tree.

Leonard then proceeded to hole his monster-sized putt, causing frenzied celebrations that saw the other US players, their wives and several American fans run onto and around the green. Had the putt secured the match, this behaviour would have been inappropriate, but as Olazábal still had his putt to stay in the match, it was utterly disgraceful. In the aftermath of the mayhem, Olazábal did his best to regain his concentration. Nevertheless, he just missed his putt, leaving the Americans to celebrate once again.

Samuel Ryder would have turned in his grave at the contention that followed. There were complaints from several of the European players about the behaviour of the Americans, including a claim that the wife of the European captain Mark James was spat at by an American spectator. The European press were no less forgiving: 'The behaviour of the American team, and not just on the 17th green, might have been juvenile, but it certainly wasn't surprising', wrote *Daily Telegraph* columnist Martin Johnson. 'This is a country which is so insular that most Americans still believe that the Second World War was won by John Wayne.'

■ 2006 saw the Ryder Cup contested in Ireland for the first time. More importantly, it saw the return to the golfing arena of the ever-likeable

Irishman Darren Clarke after the death of his wife Heather from breast cancer six weeks before, and a day before his 38th birthday. During her illness, Clarke had missed several tournaments in order to be with his family, and as a result had fallen out of the standings for automatic team qualification. Nevertheless, European captain Ian Woosnam selected the Irishman for his team as a wildcard pick, and it would prove to be a decision neither he nor his team would regret.

In spite of the unimaginable emotion for Clarke, he was a rock for his side, winning all three of his matches and helping his team to a record-equalling 18.5 to 9.5 victory (a record that would perhaps have been surpassed had fellow Irishman Paul McGinley not conceded a 25-foot birdie putt to J.J. Henry on the 18th hole in a remarkable sporting gesture that saw their singles match halved).

IT'S BEEN WON THE MOST TIMES BY:

America (24).

IT'S MADE OF:

Wood and solid gold.

HEIGHT:

43.2 cm.

WIDTH:

22.9 cm from handle to handle.

WEIGHT:

1,814 g.

MANTELPIECE KUDOS:

Forget your mantelpiece — attach it to the bonnet of your car and then park in your club captain's parking space.

CLEANING/MAINTENANCE REQUIRED:

There are any number of outfits worn by the American team down the years that would make a suitable rag for giving the cup a good buff.

PRIZE MONEY THAT COMES WITH IT:

None. Nor do the players get paid for competing. They do, however, amusingly get to keep their official team outfits.

ESSENTIAL FACTS:

■ Youngest American player to compete in a Ryder Cup: Horton Smith in 1929, aged 21 years and four days.

■ Oldest American player to compete in a Ryder Cup: Raymond Floyd in 1993, aged 51 years and twenty days. (His age didn't stop him from comprehensively beating a very in-form José María Olazábal in his singles match on the final day, however, to secure the Americans the trophy.)

■ Youngest European player to compete in a Ryder Cup: Sergio Garcia in 1999, aged nineteen years, eight months and fifteen days.

■ Oldest European player to compete in a Ryder Cup: Ted Ray in 1927, aged 50 years, two months and five days.

■ Nick Faldo has played in 46 Ryder Cup matches and scored a total of 25 points – more than any other European in the history of the Cup.

■ Billy Casper has played in 37 Ryder Cup matches and scored a total of 23½ points – more than any other American in the history of the Cup.

■ In 1973, at Muirfield, Europe's Bernard Gallacher contracted a serious stomach virus before the second-day foursomes, ensuring he couldn't play and that a replacement was required to join team-mate Brian Barnes. Peter Butler was chosen, and was summoned from his bed just an hour before his tee-time. It didn't seem to bother him particularly, though, as during the round he became the first player in the history of the Ryder Cup to record a hole-in-one.

■ At the gala dinner before the matches at the Belfry in 1989, American no-nonsense captain Raymond Floyd audaciously introduced his team as 'the twelve greatest players in the world'. Rather amusingly, it ended 14-14 – the second tie in the history of the event – and Europe retained possession of the Cup.

■ On singles matches day in 1977, at Royal Lytham and St Annes, Scotsman and three-time European captain Bernard Gallacher had his putter stolen between the practice range and the first tee. Not one for making a fuss, he went to the pro shop, bought himself another one and then used it to defeat Jack Nicklaus.

■ Tiger Woods had to play the last eleven holes of his Sunday singles match against Sweden's Robert Karlsson in 2006 without his 9-iron. The American's caddie Steve Williams slipped on a rock by the lake at the 7th hole of the K Club's Palmer Course and watched in horror as the iron plopped into the deep water. In spite of his depleted set of clubs, Woods won the match 3 and 2.

BEST KEPT:

Away from Brookline.

THE FIFA
WORLD CUP

THE FIFA WORLD CUP

AWARDED FOR WINNING:

A quadrennial international Association Football world championship tournament. Basically the most widely viewed and followed sporting event in the world. The absolute mother of all competitions.

CONTESTED BY:

198 nations from all six continents entered the qualification stages for the last World Cup, which started in December 2003. Thirty-two teams then contested the finals tournament in Germany in June 2006.

A BRIEF HISTORY:

Although FIFA (the Fédération Internationale de Football Association) was formed in 1904, it took them over a quarter of a century to initiate a true international tournament. Until then, the Olympics had been the only competition that offered real worldwide participation. However, in 1927, the Summer Olympic Games of 1932 was awarded to Los Angeles. Lack of interest in America for soccer and a disagreement between FIFA and the IOC saw the sport being dropped from the programme for the forthcoming Games. As a result FIFA, led by Jules Rimet, initiated the inaugural World Cup tournament in Uruguay in 1930, for which they commissioned French sculptor Abel Lafleur to create a new trophy. The prospect of a long trip across the Atlantic killed off any interest from Europe, however, the continent not offering a single entry a mere two months before the event. FIFA eventually persuaded teams from Romania, France, Belgium and Yugoslavia to take part. In addition, seven teams from South America and two more from North America ensured that the draw comprised thirteen nations. I think it would be fair to say that initial public interest was slightly on the partisan side: Romania's match against Peru was watched by 300 spectators, whereas the final saw 93,000 fans turn out to see their countrymen beat Argentina 4-2.

The 1930s saw the World Cup trophy contested three times, before the Second World War put it on hold for twelve years. During the war, the Vice President of FIFA, Dr Ottorino Barassi, hid it in a shoebox under his bed to stop it falling into the hands of the occupying Germans. Just after the war, in 1946, the trophy was renamed the Jules Rimet Cup as a way of honouring his inauguration of the tournament. Then, in 1966, the Cup was stolen while on display in England, only to be discovered a week later under a bush near Croydon by a dog called Pickles. Pickles became an instant celebrity, earning his owners a £3,000 reward (three times as much as each of the England players got for winning the trophy). As a security measure, FIFA then secretly made a replica, particularly for use in post-match celebrations.

As had been agreed by FIFA in 1928, the first country to win the tournament three times would get to keep the trophy. Mexico City in 1970 saw Brazil triumph for the third time and therefore get the Jules Rimet Cup permanently. FIFA immediately commissioned a new trophy for the tenth World Cup in 1974. Experts from seven countries submitted a total of 53 designs, the task finally being awarded to Italian artist Silvio Gazzaniga, who crafted the trophy that remains in use today. He said: 'I had it in my mind to create something that symbolised effort and exertion, while at the same time expressing harmony, simplicity and peace.' Unlike its predecessor, FIFA has stated that it will remain in their possession in perpetuity. The base has room for seventeen small plaques bearing the name of the winners – space enough to keep it busy until 2038. What happens to it after that remains to be seen ...

MOST MEMORABLE MOMENTS:

■ No goal has been more debated in any boozer than Geoff Hurst's second in the 1966 final against West Germany. At 2-2 in extra time, Hurst received the ball in the box, upon which he turned and shot ferociously, the ball clattering against the underside of the bar and directly down. Now, if you're German, the chances are you'll think the ball didn't cross the line, but if you're English, it's a fairly safe bet that you'll think it did. Anyway, the Swiss referee didn't know, and so had to consult his Russian linesman, who said it had crossed the line – and by doing so, did more for Anglo-Soviet relations during the Cold War than any politician.

■ In 1970, playing a Brazilian side that's widely regarded as the best football team of all time, England's goalkeeper Gordon Banks was forced to make what is without question the greatest save of all time. 'He came from nowhere', complained Pelé. 'I headed it perfectly towards one corner of the net while Banks was at the other corner. I was already shouting GOOOL!!! when Banks, like a salmon leaping up a falls, threw himself in the air and managed to tip the ball so it slid over the crossbar. It was an impossible play.' You'd struggle to get a better endorsement than that.

■ Four minutes from the end of the 1970 final against Italy, Brazil were already 3-1 ahead and cruising to their third time as champions in four tournaments. That didn't stop them then creating and scoring the best team goal the World Cup had ever seen.

It started with Brazilian centre-forward Tostão, who, having come back to help defend, regained possession in the left-back position. He then calmly passed in-field to Piazza, who then just as casually passed to Clodoaldo. Then Clodoaldo, still in his own half, danced around the challenges of four Italian players before nonchalantly passing to Rivelino. Rivelino then chipped it up to Jairzinho on the left wing. Jairzinho then cut inside and passed to Pelé, who, standing just outside Italy's box, took the ball at his feet and just stopped. He then just waited before casually, and without even looking, pushing the ball to his right. Then, seemingly from nowhere, Carlos Alberto arrived like a rocket on the right-hand side of the box and, with his first touch, leathered the ball into the far side of the net.

Three minutes later, they were champions of the world again, the pitch was invaded by adoring fans, and several of the players were stripped of everything they wore except their shorts.

■ At the 1978 World Cup, Scotland had the dubious pleasure of meeting tournament favourites Holland in the group stage. Scotland had already lost to Peru and drawn with Iran and, as a result, needed to beat the Dutch and their near-perfect brand of total football by three clear goals. They failed by a narrow margin, but not before Archie Gemmill had put Scotland 3-1 up and brought the impossible within their grasp with one of the best goals the World Cup has ever seen.

The little Scottish midfielder picked up a loose ball on the right of the Dutch box, ran backwards and then turned in-field before he drew the challenge of midfielder Wim Jansen. Jumping over the Dutchman's sliding tackle, Gemmill continued on his path towards goal, evaded the flailing and desperate tackle of Dutch captain and sweeper Rudi Krol, then nutmegged Jan Poortvliet, before finally lifting the ball over advancing goalkeeper Jan Jongbloed and into the net.

Unfortunately for Scotland, the Dutch had pulled the score back to 3-2 by the end of the game. So in spite of Gemmill's heroics and the fact that Scotland had beaten the team that went on to the final, they once again made an early exit from the competition.

■ One of the World Cup's more peculiar moments came from Welsh referee Clive Thomas at the end of a match between Brazil and Sweden in 1978. With the scores level at 1-1, the Brazilians floated in a corner kick which Zico successfully headed into the net to give the South Americans a last-gasp victory. Instead, the referee disallowed the goal, having blown the full-time whistle as the ball was in mid-air.

■ The group match between West Germany and Austria in Spain in 1982 will be remembered for all the wrong reasons. A 1-0 win to the Germans would ensure that both teams would advance to the next round at the expense of Algeria. As West Germany took the lead in the tenth minute, both sides practically stopped playing, nonchalantly passing amongst each other. Outrage in the stadium was unanimous, a German fan on the terraces even setting fire to his own national flag. Algeria immediately protested to FIFA, calling for both teams to be disqualified, but their complaint was rejected. Nevertheless, from the next World Cup to the present day, the last round of matches in the group stage have been played simultaneously to avoid any similar fiasco.

■ When West Germany met France in 1982, the world saw probably the worst tackle ever made on a football field. In the 65th minute, with the score at 1-1, French defender Patrick Battiston found himself clean through on goal. German keeper Harald Schumacher came charging off his line and, making absolutely no attempt whatsoever to play the ball, clattered into Battiston, hip-first. Battiston was carried off, lost three teeth, and required oxygen before being taken to hospital. Not only did Schumacher absolutely inexplicably not receive a card of either colour, he rather annoyingly went on to be the hero of the penalty shootout.

■ The 1982 World Cup saw probably the most bizarre incident in the tournament's history. France were leading 3-1 against Kuwait when Alain Giresse fired home France's fourth from close range as Kuwaiti defenders – thinking they had heard a whistle – remained rooted to the spot. The Kuwaiti FA President, Prince Fahid, left his seat in the stands and came charging onto the field, threatening to make his team walk off if the goal wasn't disallowed. Somewhat strangely, the Russian referee agreed, scrubbing the goal from the scoresheet, and the game continued. France went on to win 4-1.

FIFA later fined the Prince £8,000, but as one of the richest men in the world, I can't imagine he was especially bothered.

■ In 1986, Argentina and England met on a football field for the first time since the conclusion of the Falklands War four years before. To add to the fervour, it was the quarter-final of the World Cup, and whatever tension remained between the two nations led to some fighting among the 114,580 fans before the game.

Early in the second half, and with the score still 0-0, England midfielder Steve Hodge intercepted the ball as Argentine captain Diego Maradona and Jorge Valdano attempted a one-two on the edge of the English penalty area. Failing to clear, the Englishman accidentally spooned the ball into the air and also into the middle of the box, leaving goalkeeper Peter Shilton to come charging off his line in order to punch it away from the advancing Maradona. Now you would have thought that, at 5'6", it was fairly unlikely that Maradona, using his head, would be able to beat the 6'1" Shilton, who was allowed to use his hands. Well, I'm sure it would be, except that Maradona decided he could use his hands as well, tipping the ball over Shilton and into the net, giving Argentina a 1-0 lead.

In his 2002 autobiography, Maradona wrote: 'At the time I called it "the hand of God". Bollocks was it the hand of God, it was the hand of Diego! And it felt a little bit like pickpocketing the English.' More recently, in 2005, he suggested that it was a riposte for the UK's victory in the Falklands War, saying: 'Whoever robs a thief gets a 100-year pardon.'

■ Crafty as his first goal was, his second, four minutes later, is unquestionably the greatest individual goal ever scored in a World Cup.

Maradona received the ball from team-mate Héctor Enrique some ten metres inside his own half before embarking on a 60-metre waltz towards the English goal, skinning Hoddle, then Reid, then Sansom, then Butcher, then Fenwick, before slotting past a hapless and helpless Shilton. It was so utterly brilliant that a statue of Maradona immortalising the moment has since been erected outside the stadium.

■ As part of the opening ceremony of the 1994 World Cup in the USA, the singer Diana Ross took part in a choreographed routine in which she took a penalty (from four yards out) at a specially designed goal. As the ball hit the back of the net, the goal was meant to crack and split in half, the hundreds of millions of viewers being amazed by the singer's searing right foot. Unfortunately – for her anyway – her attempt went off at a right angle, missing the open goal by a mile. With the ball dribbling pathetically towards the corner flag, the goal fell apart anyway, bringing the fiasco to a beautifully fitting conclusion.

■ When Oleg Salenko arrived at the 1994 World Cup, pretty much no one outside his native Russia had heard of him. That wasn't to be the case by the time he left. Playing against the 1990 quarter-finalists Cameroon, the striker went on the rampage, slotting home five goals in one game – an individual World Cup record that saw them to a 6-1 win.

Salenko ended up sharing the golden boot with Bulgaria's Hristo Stoichov, with six goals each to their name. This was made all the more amazing by the fact that, despite their crushing of Cameroon, Russia didn't make it out of the group stage and the Bulgarian got to play an additional four matches in the tournament.

■ In 1998, England played Argentina in the second round. It was the first time the two nations had met since the bitter feud over the 'hand of God' twelve years previously, and it turned out to be the most watched match in British TV history.

About fifteen minutes into the game, an eighteen-year-old Michael Owen received a pass from David Beckham on the halfway line. Owen left everyone around him in his wake as he charged up the field. He beat José Chamot, then Roberto Ayala, before coolly curling the ball past Carlos Roa high into the net.

In just ten seconds, the teenager had announced himself on the world's biggest footballing stage.

■ The 2006 France vs. Italy World Cup final started with both teams scoring in the first twenty minutes. Frenchman Zinedine Zidane opened the scoring with a controversial penalty before Italian Marco Materazzi headed the scores level a little more than ten minutes later. The score then remained 1-1 until the end of 90 minutes, forcing the game into extra time.

During extra time, Zidane almost sealed it for the French, only to see his ferocious header brilliantly tipped over the crossbar. Then, in the 110th minute of the game, Zidane's head came into play again, but in a very different way. Off the ball, Zidane and Materazzi could be seen altercating in some way. Materazzi later suggested in an interview with an Italian sports daily that it went a little like this: 'I held his shirt for a few seconds only, he turned to me, looked at me from top to bottom with utmost arrogance and said: "If you really want my shirt, I'll give it to you afterwards." I answered him with an insult.' Now, never in the history of the human race has the content of an insult been considered, examined, dissected, studied and generally analysed the world over. News agencies from around the world hired in professional lip-readers and Italian translators to try to ascertain from the TV footage what Materazzi had said.

After exhaustive studies of the footage in the following days, the general consensus was that Materazzi had called Zidane 'the son of a terrorist whore', before adding 'so just f*** off' for good measure. Although the finer details of the colourful exchange between the two players will perhaps never be known, we do know that it provoked what would turn out to be Zidane's last-ever action as a professional footballer. Zidane, who was seen to be walking away from the conversation, stopped, turned around and walked over to Materazzi before head-butting the Italian in the chest so hard it knocked him over. The referee consequently showed Zidane a red card.

As the Frenchman left a professional football field for the very last time, we witnessed what will turn out to be one of the most enduring images of any World Cup: removing his captain's armband, the crestfallen star walked past the trophy that had been set up on a plinth beside the pitch; a trophy that, but for his moment of madness, would probably have been his. In the most unbefitting way possible, world football said goodbye to one of the greatest players it had ever seen.

IT'S BEEN WON THE MOST TIMES BY:

Brazil – 5. Italy – 4. Germany – 3.

IT'S MADE OF:

Malachite and solid 18-carat gold.

HEIGHT:

36.8 cm.

WEIGHT:

6,175 g.

MANTELPIECE KUDOS:

Unrivalled. I'm not sure they've invented a mantelpiece that deserves it yet.

INSURANCE VALUE:

100,000 Swiss francs.

ESSENTIAL FACTS:

■ In 1990 the United Arab Emirates scored two goals. Although only in the group stage, the scorers celebrated as if they had won the whole thing. That might have had something to do with the Rolls-Royce they were going to receive on their return home for every goal they had scored.

■ 1.5 billion people watched the 2002 final on TV. In other words, one in every four people on the entire planet. 300 million people even tuned in to watch the 2006 preliminary group stage team draw.

■ In the 1962 World Cup in Chile, Brazil played England in the quarter-finals and won 3-1. During the game, a stray dog ran onto the pitch. The canine successfully evaded all attempts by the players to capture it, until England striker Jimmy Greaves got down on all fours to beckon it over. Although he was successful in catching the dog, the animal's parting shot before leaving the field was to urinate all over Greaves's England shirt.

Brazilian star and double goal-scorer in the game, 'Little Bird' Garrincha, found the incident so amusing that he took the dog home as a pet.

■ The 2006 World Cup in Germany saw a record number of bookings: 345 yellow cards and 28 red cards were brandished, the match between Holland and Portugal alone accounting for sixteen and four respectively.

■ 199,854 people squeezed into the Maracana stadium in Rio de Janeiro to see the 1950 final – still the World Cup's biggest-ever attendance.

■ The World Cup has been held eighteen times. Of the ten contested in Europe, only one saw victory by a non-European side (Brazil in Sweden in 1958). In stark contrast, when staged outside Europe, the tournament has been won only by South American sides.

Only two nations from outside these two continents have ever reached the semi-finals: the USA (1930) and South Korea (2002).

■ In 1994, as a result of scoring an own goal during a 2-1 defeat at the hands of the USA, Colombian defender Andrés Escobar was murdered on his return to his country, shot repeatedly in the street. There was similar fervour in a Thai household in 2002, when a man shot his wife for changing the channel while he was watching England's second-round match with Denmark. In the words of the late Bill Shankly: 'Some people believe football is a matter of life and death. I'm very disappointed with that attitude. I can assure you it is much, much more important than that.'

BEST KEPT:

Where your wife normally sleeps.